MW00386767

Heal Thy Self

*Tapping Your Innate Wisdom to Heal
Your Mind, Body, and Spirit*

Powerful You!
PUBLISHING
Sharing Wisdom ~ Shining Light

HEAL THY SELF
Tapping Your Innate Wisdom to Heal
Your Mind, Body, and Spirit

Copyright © 2017

All rights reserved. No part of this book may be reproduced by any mechanical, photographic, or electronic process, or in the form of a phonographic recording; nor may it be stored in a retrieval system, transmitted, or otherwise copied for public or private use–other than for "fair use" as brief quotations embodied in articles and reviews–without prior written permission of the publisher.

The authors of this book do not dispense medical advice or prescribe the use of any technique as a form of treatment for physical, emotional, or medical problems without the advice of a physician, either directly or indirectly. Nor is this book intended to provide personalized legal, accounting, financial, or investment advice. Readers are encouraged to seek the counsel of competent professionals with regards to such matters. The intent of the authors is to provide general information to individuals who are taking positive steps in their lives for emotional and spiritual well-being. If you use any of the information in this book for yourself, which is your constitutional right, the authors and the publisher assume no responsibility for your actions.

Published by: Powerful You! Inc. USA
powerfulyoupublishing.com

Library of Congress Control Number: 2017939743

Sue Urda and Kathy Fyler–First Edition

ISBN: 978-0-9970661-5-9

First Edition June 2017

Body, Mind & Spirit: Healing

Printed in the United States of America

Dedication

*This book is dedicated to everyone
committed to a self-healing journey.
As you seek, so you shall find.*

Table of Contents

May You Live Each Day Open to Possibility...

And May You Heal Thy Self!

Foreword

When I was asked to write the foreword for Sue Urda and Kathy Fyler's newest anthology, I was so honored and excited to be able to share my thoughts with you. Sue and Kathy are two very special friends and colleagues of mine. I met them years ago after they launched their wonderful organization, Powerful You! and after attending my first meeting at a local chapter, I was so impressed with the energy and vibe of their networking group that I became a facilitator of my own chapter to be able to reach more women and expand this phenomenal network of conscious, loving and powerful women.

I was also a contributing author in their first anthology where I shared my own personal story about my weight loss journey that took me to age 40, back in 2004, to finally get a handle on. Like many of you who are reading this book, I have had my own health struggles and challenges and to be able to overcome those issues, is what shaped me and my ability to assist others on their journey too.

As a holistic health professional for the past 30 years, their newest book *Heal Thy Self, Tapping Your Innate Wisdom to Heal Your Mind, Body, and Spirit*, really speaks and emanates my language and philosophy about what it takes to be truly well; physically, mentally, emotionally, and spiritually too. My husband and I were pioneers, opening up the very first holistic health center in our area, back in 1989. As chiropractors, we are taught that the power that made the body can heal the body and that is something I have witnessed first hand for over 3 decades. I know and believe this to be true.

As you will read in the various chapters of this incredible book, no matter where people are on their healing journey and no matter how hard the struggle may be to truly become healthy and live a life of optimal, vibrant, and total health, it is absolutely possible. However, it takes an approach that incorporates the 'whole' person. It is unfortunate that in our society today and in our traditional medical community, there are 'specialists' for everything. When you have a problem with your heart, you are expected to seek the advice of a cardiologist; one who specializes in cardiovascular disease. When you have a problem with your thyroid, you are expected to seek the advice of an endocrinologist; one who specializes in endocrine related disease. These types of specialists will typically run some blood work and then prescribe a particular medication (or many medications) to 'control' your symptoms rather than correct the actual cause of the disease. When you are feeling anxious and depressed, you are expected to see a psychiatrist and be prescribed anti-depressants and anti-anxiety medications as opposed to really addressing the underlying cause of why you are feeling that way to begin with. Don't get me wrong, I am not saying that there isn't a time or a place for orthodox medicine or to seek the advice of traditional medical professionals, but so many of the health conditions and diseases that are prevalent in our society today are caused by poor diet, an overload of stress, toxins in our environment, unhealthy lifestyle habits, and other factors that need to be addressed and handled in order for our bodies to rebalance and allow us to truly heal on all levels.

Each and every one of us are unique and have our own distinct differences. When it comes to healing, there is 'no one size fits all' protocol. There are many factors and influences involved in true healing and attaining optimal health and wellness. As a chiropractor and a nutritionist, it's quite obvious to me that nutrition and spinal health play a significant role in healing, and it goes without saying that mindset and getting back to the basics of a healthy lifestyle are all important in assisting people on their healing journey. It's also obvious that we need to address our emotions. Anger, resentment, grief, blame, regret, and other similar emotions can also play a huge role in our physical well-being and overall health. Without addressing these underlying areas, it's impossible to truly attain the level of health and vitality that we desire.

However, even if we just talk about nutrition for a moment, we all know that there is not a single eating plan or dietary style that works for everyone. We all come to this earth with biochemical individuality which makes us each unique in our specific nutritional needs. So what works for one person doesn't necessarily work for the next. This is a perfect example of tapping your own innate wisdom. When we tune in to our innate intelligence and let that guide us to what is right for us both physically, as well as on a mental and spiritual level too, we can be guided down the right path. Too often in our society, people will hand over their own responsibility to their 'doctor'. They will give their personal power away.

First and foremost, we must realize that we *can* "heal thyself". We can tap into that powerful inner wisdom. We can tune in and listen to our inborn knowledge of what we need to do for our own healing and how we need to be to achieve and continue to attain abundant health. Health is our absolute greatest wealth and as my sweet grandmother always said, if you don't have your health, you have nothing. So, tap in, tune in and make your health your #1 priority. Let your inner wisdom guide you to heal your body, mind and spirit!

With love and gratitude,

Dr. Ina Nozek, DC, MS

Introduction

So often when we open the pages of a book, we wonder what we will find. There is great excitement and anticipation as we hold the book in our hands, read the title, or simply immerse ourselves in the cover image. Our expectation causes changes even before we read the pages of the book. We begin to alchemize and shift in our thinking, our bodies, and in our spirit. As many of the authors in this book will attest, the same is true of the healing process.

The stories in this book explore the lives and experiences of many strong and heart-centered women who have the common intention to help others on their own journey of healing. Some stories show that healing takes years, months, or weeks depending on the depth of the 'injury' and the state of the individual; while others show that healing happens in the exact moment when the mind, heart, and spirit are ready for it.

You might be wondering how a book like this comes together. More accurately, you may wish to know how a group of women from all over North America—many who don't know each other and may never even meet in person—have conspired to bring forth such a book.

You might wonder why they would bare their souls, expose their secrets, and show you their flaws.

You might ask who would share such deeply personal and sometimes unflattering truths about themselves. Who would air their 'dirty laundry' or put themselves up for possible ridicule, judgment, and scrutiny? Why go there if you don't have to? Why not keep it tucked away in a closet somewhere and go on living your life?

The answer is simple…

These women have stepped into their personal power and realized that there is no shame in the journey.

As you read the stories you will see the raw emotion and unbridled heart of each author. You will share in her joys and her pain; you will laugh, cry, and celebrate with her. Her story may reflect your own, and through her transformation, you will gain insights and strength, courage and freedom.

You may see your "Self" in some of these stories.

These are ordinary women, like you, who have transformed their circumstances into something personally extraordinary. They trusted their intuition, tapped their innate knowing, and followed their inner guidance. The evidence is in the lives they live today.

It takes a village, not only to raise a child, but to raise ourselves into the women we would have ourselves become.

It is the wish and intent of these authors to be authentic and truthful with themselves and others so they may move forward powerfully in life, having learned and grown from their mistakes, triumphs, and experiences—and if *they* can do it, *you* can too! Many of these authors have careers and businesses that focus on assisting other women to heal, grow, and empower themselves, and all of them have chosen to share their story in the hopes of helping someone like you along the way.

It is said that you must release the past before you can fully live the potential for your life. It would appear this is a powerful first step.

Allow yourself to become immersed in these stories and learn the lessons that are shared—they may help you to move forward from the beliefs that hold you from your healing. Allow yourself to believe that healing is possible for you. We know the placebo effect is real, and your own belief can be more powerful than any medicine. In these stories, you will find comfort, guidance, and joy. And surely you will find hope. May you also find personal meaning for yourself within these pages, and may the heartfelt words of these authors serve as a beacon of strength for your journey.

There is no right or wrong way to heal yourself. Choose whatever resonates with you, whatever feels good to you, and above all, trust the process.

It is our intention and purpose to be a source for good and to do our part in raising consciousness and compassion in the world. This book contributes to this purpose.

Know above all that you can be, do, and have anything you desire—these women are living proof. And if you ever need encouragement, inspiration, or hope, simply flip through the book, open any page, and read. Your heart will open and expand, and you will be served on your journey of healing.

Wishing you ease, peace, and vibrant well-being...

With gratitude and love,

Sue Urda & Kathy Fyler

Let the Healing Begin

"Love is the great miracle cure.
Loving ourselves works miracles in our lives."
~ Louise L. Hay

Truth's Memory
Francie Canter

In a tender moment of awareness
a memory of truth emerges
in the presence of now
recollecting the past.

Did it have to be so painful?

Where the experience became the teacher
through the other side of trauma.
Where the trauma was the falling apart of everything
believed to be true.

Where the heart so hurt becomes strengthened
through passages in time and teachings
evolving
reuniting
in its truth
becoming the way
to know

Be still my mind, my thoughts, my past

My worries, fears, remembrances
Remember   Truths Now Known
Remember Truth
Remember.

No matter what is happening
No matter what is said
Faith's choice within creates and
Practice of allows

Breathe

          Breathe

                    Breathe

Open hope
in peace
limitless
in greater good for all

ABOUT THE AUTHOR: With gratitude and in honor of the rare and gifted teachers met along the way, Francie founded Visionary Legends of Love Inc, a 501(c)(3) nonprofit organization so that many more may be aware of and receive the works and teachings of these legendary individuals.

Francie Canter
Visionary Legends of Love, Inc
A 501c3 nonprofit organization
visionarylegends@gmail.com

Remember Your Toolbox
Ruth Kent

At various times in my life, people—usually experts in their respective field—have said to me, "I'm sorry, there is nothing more we can do for you." They have said it with regard to my physical, emotional, and financial health, and every time I heard it, I felt helpless, scared, not good enough, rejected and, at times, stupid. I would step into what I referred to as "Limbo Land," a place of prolonged uncertainty. For many years I spent quite a bit of time there, until I received the tools that would bring healing to every facet of my life.

In 1996, I was a forty-five-year-old Intensive Care Nurse in San Diego; married to an amazing man, and mother to a beautiful, vivacious five-year-old girl. I was blessed in so many ways, yet I couldn't seem to rid myself of the constant, severe pain I was in, or even determine the cause. I had gone to chiropractors, acupuncturists, a doctor of nutrition, internists, a rheumatoid specialist, an Energy Zoning therapist, and a pulmonologist. They came up with plenty of diagnoses: autoimmune imbalance, arthritis, allergy-induced asthma, degenerative joint disease, and various neuromuscular challenges, but they could never seem to pinpoint the root cause of these problems. I gave each of their programs at least six months, hoping to see the situation improve. To me, these treatments were like climbing a ladder—for a while I would seem to be "climbing the rungs"—then suddenly I would stop responding to the program, start having reactions to the treatment, and slide down the ladder from wellness to disease again. I felt there was something I was missing, some emotional thread that needed to be cut, but I could not figure out what it was. Still, throughout the ordeal, I kept hearing *be positive, hold the faith, stay focused, and all good will come.*

One day, while sitting in a doctor's office and nearly at the end of my rope, I asked God to show me what I needed. After reviewing my file the doctor said those familiar words: "There is nothing we can do for you." He then predicted that within six years I would be in a wheelchair. Surgery was not the answer, either. With all the degenerations, herniation, and misalignments in my back, I would need not one operation, but several. It was not, he said, a safe option, but it was my decision to make. As I tried to absorb this information, the doctor stopped speaking and reached into a bottom drawer of his desk. It was during this brief pause that a profound sense of calmness came over me; it was as if I was observing everything as a third person in the room. Suddenly, I knew with absolute certainty that I needed to go home and pray.

The doctor placed some forms in front of me. They were Disability papers, he said, so I could apply for financial assistance. Certainly, this would be helpful, but it was not the answer I was looking for.

After my appointment I went home and prayed for three days. Honestly, I could not tell you anything else that took place during that time. By now my physical condition had deteriorated even further—I had lost the medial and lateral nerve path of my left leg, and was unable to work at the hospital or even do light housework. My dear husband was working full-time and doing all the cleaning, grocery shopping, and laundry. Eventually, it became too much and we got a housekeeper to help out. Our savings were being depleted. Yet, after those three days of praying I felt I had reached an overall feeling of what I refer to as "Comfortable Confidence."

Comfortable Confidence is a term I find best describes the feeling when all is in alignment, physically, emotionally, and spiritually with the Divine source (God). A sense of inner peace is present. I made a decision to know and believe that everything has a solution. I began to focus on what I was asking to achieve, be open to the guidance, and trust that whatever I need to be aware of will be shown to me. At that moment, I no longer owned the pain, fears, doubts, and limitations. It was if I was being taken by the hand and supported unconditionally. I was ready to have the story change. My heart was wide open, vulnerable, and excited—about what, I did not know exactly—I just knew I was agreeing to get and *be* better.

Shortly thereafter, I was invited to a gathering of one of my patients. Getting there wasn't easy because of my physical challenges, which were exacerbated by any car ride longer than twenty minutes. I finally arrived and found the room packed with people, good food, and music. I happened to mention that I would love to dance, and the lady across the table asked me why I wasn't.

"Right now it is not possible," I replied, "my left leg can't move correctly and my back does not tolerate this activity either."

She looked at me for a moment, then said, "I have the answer for you."

When she mentioned the name Nikken, Inc., I immediately knew this was something I needed to know about. The feeling would simply not let go of me, so I went to an event showcasing the products. Nikken, I found out, is a wellness company whose products put your body in the right environment to boost your own innate healing. Finally, something other than, "Sorry there is nothing we can do for you."

There was, however, the very real issue of cost to consider. When I asked my husband what I should do, he didn't hesitate. "We have to do this," he said.

Three days after charging the products on our credit card, he ran into the house, excitedly yelling for me. He was smiling from ear to ear and waving a piece of paper. I took a look at it and gasped—it was a bonus check from his job, and enough to cover the cost of the products, and then some.

Within a couple of months I got to know some of the people at Nikken, and several of them, after hearing my story, said, "Oh, you have to meet Dr. Bradley Nelson."

Dr. Nelson was a chiropractor who also did energy work. I didn't know whether he could help me, but by then I'd learned to trust the information I was receiving. I soon began seeing him three times a week. Dr. Nelson introduced me to his work, The Emotion Code and Body Code work. These modalities focus on releasing trapped negative energy that sometimes manifest as physical conditions. As he spoke, I was overcome with the feeling that this was about helping patients get to the core of the problem, rather than just treating their symptoms. Traditional medicine did not focus on this, but I knew from listening to my patients—especially those with cancer—that there was always some loss, event, and/or emotions they experienced around the time their disease appeared. I figured I would give it a chance—at that point, what did I have to lose?

I began religiously using the products, releasing negative emotions with The Emotion Code and Body Code, and visualizing myself as healthy and happy. Within three and a half months, I was pain-free, standing upright, and had even started exercising again. I was also able to go back to work; most importantly, I was able to be a wife and mother again.

In 2008, I would reconnect with Dr. Nelson, albeit for a very different reason. While my physical health was good, I had for some time felt overwhelmed by a combination of financial burdens and my responsibilities at home and work. It was even causing strain on my marriage.

Dr. Nelson did an Emotion Code session with me, the intention of which was to release any trapped emotions that were contributing to the challenges in my marriage. Following this session I felt peaceful and more grounded again, like I could focus on possibilities, not the problems. Though I said nothing to my husband about this session, he noticed something different in me.

"You seem more at ease," he commented, "and not so uptight about things."

The session—and my husband's validation—had reminded me that when we focus on what we want and are open and guided to receive, the answers will show up, even if they don't look the way we think they will. I also realized that over the years I'd kept the tools that helped me heal physically on a shelf, using them only occasionally.

I started utilizing The Emotion Code and Body Code methods in my daily life, and I soon noticed that the head chatter was gone, replaced by a sense of inner peace and a knowing that somehow, someway, all would be okay. At the same time, my inner voice— my intuition—also became much easier to hear. I clearly recall saying, "This is what joy feels like." It was amazing!

After seeing how The Emotion Code changed my life, I started thinking that maybe I should learn to do it for other people. One day, while sitting at my desk, I asked God, "If this is truly what you wish for me to do, than give me a snow cone in the forehead. I don't want a sign. I want to know without a doubt that this is what you are asking of me." As if on cue, the phone started ringing, and I thought to myself, if this is God I am hanging up. Well, it wasn't God, but a friend of mine. "Hey," she said, "Are you going to Chicago for The Emotion Code Seminar?"

Considering what I had just said to God, I was a bit taken aback by the question. "Actually, I was thinking about it, why do you ask?"

"I'd like to pay for your trip," she replied.

I felt a sensation in the middle of my forehead and knew I was meant to go.

"Thank you for being obedient," I replied, "God and I will take care of the rest." As I said the words, I felt like someone was speaking right through me; I knew there was a bigger purpose that I was only coming to know.

From there, everything fell into place—I got an affordable flight to Chicago and found a roommate; food was provided by those holding the class. God had certainly responded to my question with a resounding yes! In 2008 I became certified in The Emotion Code, and 2010 I became certified in The Body Code.

The year 2010 also had its challenges, however. Facing bankruptcy, my husband and I made the decision to move out of our house. Why was this happening? We didn't know, and neither did the financial consultant, who stated, "There is nothing else we can do for you. This is the only answer. You have done all you can do." Back in Limbo Land once again, I did what was necessary—I became unattached to stuff, asked for help from above every day, and used the tools. I also remained in gratitude for what was working. My husband and I were communicating and getting along much better, and I was feeling healthy, inside and out.

During the process of moving, I received another tool. I was cleaning off a shelf when suddenly on my lap there appeared a piece of paper. Where in the world had it come from? I looked around but had no idea. I looked more closely at it and realized it had been typed on an old ribbon typewriter. The note read:

Dear Ruth,

Do what is necessary, then what is possible and soon you will find yourself doing the impossible.

~St. Francis of Assisi

Once again, I had opened my heart to guidance and God had provided reassurance that all would improve. The tools God gave me have taken me from surviving to thriving in all areas of my life: spiritually, physically, mentally, emotionally, creatively, and financially. No matter what challenges you are facing, there is always a solution, always a way to find our way to a path of love, joy, gratitude, and freedom. It is our divine birthright, we need only claim it. We need only to Stop—Pause and Pray.

ABOUT THE AUTHOR: Ruth Kent, RN, CBCP, is an Emotion Code Seminar Instructor and the creator of the Success Together Program. She has worked in healthcare for nearly five decades, forty-one of them as an Intensive Care nurse; however, it was her physical, emotional, and financial struggles that served as the catalyst for spiritual growth and expanded her abilities to help others. A series of synchronicities led her to the work of Dr. Bradley Nelson and a profound transformation. Today, she provides her clients with simple self-help tools that support them where they are and provide the means to live a life of joy through freedom.

Ruth Kent, RN, CBCP
ruthkentllc.com
Mobile: 828-778-0254
Home: 828-298-2718
Ruthkentpresent@gmail.com

Baby David
Karen Schaaf

I was on my way to work when I went into labor with Baby David. As a social worker, my schedule was quite hectic; in fact, just a few days earlier, my supervisor, amazed that I was not taking any time off before the birth, jokingly he asked if I was one of those women who gave birth in a rice paddy and immediately went back to work. I smiled and said yes, but really I wanted to spend the six weeks I had squirreled away with my newborn. When the first contraction hit, I went home and timed them until they were three or four minutes apart, then asked my husband to take me to the hospital. I later delivered a healthy baby boy we named David Jesse.

I loved being home with Baby David and his two older siblings. In most ways, David was just like his brother and sister had been at that age, though he did sleep more. When he was about five weeks old, I was rocking him to sleep when I started to "hear" very disturbing thoughts coming from him—statements like "hit me" and "hurt me." Immediately I realized he was spiritually sick, and after getting him to sleep, I laid him on my bed, then placed four crystals around his tiny body to create a medicine circle. I then sat with him in the circle and prayed for God and Christ to heal my son.

A week later, I decided it was time for him to start sleeping in the bassinette in his older sister's room, instead of in bed with me and my husband. That night, after dinner and his bath, I laid him in his bassinette, on his side in case he spit up. In the middle of the night, I woke to the sound of crying. I got up and started down the hall to his room, but as soon as I opened his door he stopped crying and I turned around and went back to bed.

When I woke the next morning I immediately knew something

was wrong. I ran into my son's room and reached down to him. His body was cold and stiff and white foam was coming from his nose. I screamed for my husband, who came running into the room. He held David and cried while I called 911. A few minutes later we were sitting in the living room as medical personnel examined him. It was surreal. When they were done, I asked the police if I could hold my son for a while. They said yes, so I took him and sat on my daughter's bed. I did what I'd always done when facing difficult situations: I started to pray.

I remembered the Bible stories of Christ raising the dead, and I begged Him now to do the same for David. I kept thinking if my faith was strong enough, my son would return to me. Finally, when nothing happened, I went back into the living room and handed him to the coroner. As soon as the police and medical personnel left I broke down in hysterics. I could not believe God would do this to me.

Determined to find out what had happened, I spoke with the coroner who performed the autopsy. She could not find anything physically wrong with David and determined that he had died of SIDS. I later learned that SIDS is still a mystery to the medical community. Sometimes, perfectly healthy children just stop breathing, and for some reason, it is more common among Native American children. Though it was good to have this information, it didn't make the loss any easier to accept.

My husband and I then began the agonizing process of planning our son's funeral. We decided to have Baby David cremated, and arranged a Catholic showing of his ashes at the funeral home for friends and family; a second ceremony was at my parent's property, overlooking the Puget Sound. When it came to the burial, we decided upon a Native American service.

David's ashes were placed in a decorative gourd, and the medicine woman called "J" conducted the burial ceremony. Per her request, my husband and I dug a hole three feet deep and three feet across; we also brought toys, clothes, and food for Baby David. Standing barefoot in the hole, J started to drum and sing a song. When she was finished, she climbed out of the hole and had my husband place the gourd with David's ashes inside it, then step on it to crush the gourd and ashes into the ground. J then built a fire on top of the broken gourd, and asked that we step forward with the toys and other items she'd requested. These things we would place into the fire to send to David on the other side. I went first, with an outfit, blanket, and baby formula and placed or poured them in the fire. Each item burnt up in a large blue flame. My husband was next, placing a toy and pajamas in the pile of burning items; he was followed by my daughter and son, who along with other family and friends, placed their own items in the fire.

J picked up her drum again, and as she sang to Baby David, a baby bald eagle flew over the cliff by the inlet and landed on a large fir tree. This baby eagle sat on this large tree looking over us. As soon as the ceremony ended, it flew off across the waters of Puget Sound, and I knew without a doubt that my son had been watching us though his eyes.

I went back to work but found it very difficult, especially when dealing with abuse cases. All I wanted was to have my child back, and there were people who were basically throwing theirs away! It was too much to deal with. I met with J and requested a sweat lodge ceremony, hoping to find out why Baby David had been taken from me. I had not even been able to communicate with Spirit, for I felt they had punished and abandoned me.

Sweat lodges differ in appearance from tribe to tribe. Mine— the Chippewa or Ojibwe of Minnesota, use birch bark. The lodges are generally round with a hole in the center so the smoke can go out the top. Inside, a deep hole is dug in the center and a fire is built. Pads or blankets are laid down around the fire, reaching to the back wall. After people take their seats, water is poured on the fire to create steam, then everyone drums and sings songs. They also pray, talk to Spirit, and wait for answers.

The answers I received were from my grandfather-in-spirit. He told me that before I left spirit I chose to give birth to Baby David. He also told me that Baby David's death had more to do with him than with me. David had lived one previous life, and was murdered as an infant. He'd been so traumatized by this death that he was afraid to incarnate again. Though brief, his life with us had been full of love; it had also corrected the imbalance in the "universal energy of ying/yang" caused by his previous death. Finally, Grandfather confirmed that David had indeed been inside the baby eagle and was very honored by our ceremony.

At the end of the sweat lodge I created tobacco ties to help me connect to Baby David. As the weeks and months passed, while in meditation I could see him growing up quickly in spirit, and he soon became a strong, young man with curly hair. Grandfather told me that David had chosen to greet children who had been murdered while in physical form and help them through their trauma. I like to refer to this as "being in the family business." I was on this side protecting children and he was on the other side, greeting the children-in-spirit who had been killed.

About a year after Baby David died, I gave birth to our youngest son, Dyl. When I later spoke to Grandfather, he reported that David was so concerned about our grief he asked his best friend-in-spirit to incarnate into our new son. Bright-eyed and exuberant, Dyl brought us a joy I thought I would never feel again. Of course, my heart still grieves the loss of David. When I asked why he left so fast, Grandfather said that "he only needed to be here for a short time."

Since then I have learned to surrender things I have no control over to God, spirit and the universe. After years of battling the universe to protect children, I finally asked God that He not place any children I could not help in my path. After this conversation, my cases flowed differently. As if by magic, things I needed to do my work suddenly appeared. I worked very hard, protecting hundreds of children, and finally retired after twenty-five years of service.

By then I had already branched out in other directions. I trained to be a Guardian ad Litem so I could represent children in custody cases. I also studied at the Hypnosis Motivation Institute in Tarzana, California and became a certified hypnotherapist.

Through my own journey work around the death of Baby David, I learned that we incarnate in this dimension to have the physical experiences we agreed to while in spirit. While we are here, Mother Earth feeds, clothes, and shelters us; She also radiates a healing and balancing energy that we can tap into, just as we connect to God's light and love that is already a part of us. I was told by Grandfather to imagine God as an endless ocean of love and light. When you were created, God placed a drop of His/ Her energy into you. This is what is meant by the phrase, "As above, so below."

Grandfather told me that I am one of many light workers walking Mother Earth right now. Our work benefits all creatures— animals and humans alike—that are slowly increasing in their vibration. This is part of a larger ascension process Grandfather calls "the change."

In my light work and meditations, I have been drawn back to my previous life as a shaman. I remember my home, which was positioned on the east side of a hill and I could greet the sun each morning. Nearby was a cave, where I would sit quietly in order to gain information for my tribe. This reconnection to my past, and to Mother Earth, has changed my life in numerous ways. Recently, I have been guided to create beautiful gemstone necklaces, the center of which are powerful amulets of Jasper and Agates. In the past, amulets of specific gemstones were used in healing and balancing our energies; now I create them so people can have direct access to Mother Earth in their daily lives. Each necklace will undergo a cleaning ceremony in a medicine wheel to make sure they are vibrating with love and light and not holding onto any denser energy.

I've also written a short book, *Medicine Jewelry: Working With Rock People,* that will accompany each necklace and earring set. It will explain which gemstones are in that particular necklace and the positive properties they contain. The book will also provide specific information on how we can clean out our chakras, and have our physical body vibrating faster, with more light and love energy. Most importantly, it discusses the universal Law of Attraction, and how through gratitude we can bring more of what we want into our lives. First, though, we must release all things from the past that do not serve us. Emotional baggage makes us feel heavy and disempowered; however, after releasing these negative images into the pillar of light running through our chakras, we start to feel lighter in mind, body, and spirit. We still remember past events, but we're no longer be triggered into having a negative response.

I am deeply grateful to Baby David for helping me rediscover my spiritual path. I understand that he came here in physical form for as long as he needed, then returned home, just as we all will one day. Mother Earth is not home, but a vacation spot and a school, designed to help us remember our true nature as beings of love and light. My son reminded me of this, and now I remind others.

ABOUT THE AUTHOR: Karen Schaaf, MA, CHt, has dedicated her life to healing and uplifting others. For over two decades she advocated for children as a Social Worker and Guardian ad Litem, and served as an independent Tribal Liaison between Native American tribes and Washington State. Today Karen has a private hypnotherapy practice, where she draws on her previous life as a Native American shaman to help others release emotional baggage and heal their lives. She also creates powerful amulets of Jasper and Agates designed to balance the wearer's energies and reconnect them to Mother Earth. Each piece of jewelry is accompanied by her book, *Medicine Jewelry: Working With Rock People.*

Karen Schaaf, MA, CHt
Big Bear Hypnotherapy & Counseling, LLC
Bigbearshypnosis4u@comcast.net
360-789-5971

Know Thy Soul, Heal Thyself in Christ

Christina Ann Sullivan

What is the soul? People have been asking that question since the beginning of time, but they often ask from the wrong perspective. We are not a body that happens to have a soul, but a soul embodied for a physical experience on this plane. The soul is our senses, desires, appetites, affections, and wounds. The soul is the core essence of our being and what resides in the soul is also what creates our personality. The hurts that we experience create deep wounds within our soul which then manifest into our behavior. The soul is where we connect to spirit, where we connect to the Holy Trinity—The Father, Son, and the Holy Spirit. That said, we all have the free will to ignore God and try to do things our way. I know, because I did this for much of my life. It was only when I truly came to know my soul and open up to a relationship with Christ that I was able to heal.

I grew up in Queens, New York, in a home that gave new meaning to the word dysfunctional. My father was extremely abusive, and although I was a very loving child, always trying to do good, I always managed to set off the time bomb inside him. One day, as I was helping him put groceries away, he flew into a rage and hit me so hard I flew across the room and smacked my head on the kitchen table. It seemed my willingness to help only enraged him, and in my child's mind, this meant I must be inherently bad and deserving of punishment.

Though I was raised Catholic, the religion rarely brought me comfort; in fact, those early experiences at church seemed to be a reflection of my home life, with sermons that painted everyone as unworthy sinners, with little hope of redemption. God sounded a lot like my own wrathful father, full of condemnation for His creation. Unlike like my father, though, God resided somewhere up in sky and out of my reach.

Still, I prayed to this God to save my mom and me from the violence and take us somewhere safe, but my prayers were never answered. My mom always kept her faith and trust that God would see us through the hard times, while I tried to find my own way out of the pain. I escaped through drugs and alcohol, and defied my parents at every turn. I also rebelled against God by turning my back on Him and Jesus. Through it all the concept of heaven and hell weighted heavily on my mind. In my teen years, I overly identified with my body, and was terribly fearful of dying. Just the thought of being buried in the ground, trapped in darkness for all eternity, terrified me. It was my version of hell.

Dysfunctional relationships clouded my mind almost as much as the substance abuse. After years of being conflicted about my sexuality, I began living as a gay woman; however, instead of feeling free I suffered rejection, discrimination, and judgement. My childhood abuse had me in a perpetual state of fight or flight, and that's how I lived, fighting to survive in this world by my wits alone, with no reliance on God. It wasn't that I no longer believed in Jesus; I just made the choice to keep him at a distance. The church had also left a powerful imprint on my mind, and I ran from it and from religion because surely, I would go to hell for who I was and all that I had done.

In my late twenties, after years of being angry with the world, my father, and God, I finally came to the realization that I alone was responsible for my self-destruction. If this was the case, it stood to reason that I must also be responsible for my own transformation. And thus began the most exciting period of my life.

I started working with various practitioners of Reiki, Akashic Record readings, past life regressions, astrological readings and spiritual coaching all over the country. These modalities helped me explore my soul while discovering my patterns and behaviors. It was like looking at a blueprint of my life and connecting the dots to see how the themes had played out. I also, for the first time, became deeply connected to my soul. The soul is like a diamond—multifaceted and often difficult to access; it is only when we dive deeply into this inner world that we discover our wounds. I held a deep "father wound" that had created a lack of self-control and, when triggered, led me to drink, eat, or spend in excess. I could also be over-reactive to people and circumstances around me. After years of living in darkness, just being aware of this wound felt close to a healing.

With each teacher and modality, I felt as though I had taken leaps and bounds in my personal and spiritual development. I awakened to my soul and gained the ability to discern between it and the ego-self. I was connected to everything and felt God's presence in it all. In fact, the transformation was so profound that I became certified in the same modalities so that I could help to serve others transform their own lives. Yet, somehow, even after all the inner work, I would still find myself falling off track time and time again. Something was missing, but what? I began asking myself questions like, *Do I identify with this person I think I am? Am I made up of all the things I have done? What is my relationship with God?*

Anyone reading this has probably asked themselves at least one of these questions at some point in their lives. The truth is, we all have a past, we have made bad choices and mistakes, we have all had heartbreak, we have regrets, and we have all felt unworthy. We are all saints and we are all sinners as well, but not in the way we have been taught to believe. We are all saints because we have Christ within us; we sin when we rebel against God's will for us and when we value the material world more than we value having a true relationship with Him.

Unbeknownst to me, this was what I was doing, even as I followed my "spiritual path." I, or more accurately, my ego, believed I could leave God out of the equation and do what I thought was best. I had been building my house on sand and not on solid rock.

"Everyone then who hears these words of mine and does them will be like a wise man who built his house on the rock. And the rain fell, and the floods came, and the winds blew and beat on that

house, but it did not fall, because it had been founded on the rock. And everyone who hears these words of mine and does not do them will be like a foolish man who built his house on the sand. And the rain fell, and the floods came, and the winds blew and beat against that house, and it fell, and great was the fall of it." ~ Matthew 7:24-27

A solid foundation is founded through true relationship to God and opening ourselves to relationship with Jesus. In examining my own resistance, I realized that although I had forgiven others for hurting me, I was still keeping Jesus at arm's length. But why? Maybe I was still punishing myself for all the things I had done or felt my sexuality deemed me unholy. After some deep reflection and contemplation, coupled with an intense desire for relationship with Christ, I decided to dive more deeply into my Catholic roots. I resolved to show up to Jesus just as I am: a "magnificent mess." For the next year, without fail, I went to the adoration chapel at church and in this safe, sacred space sat in prayer and stillness for one to two hours each day. My experiences during adoration were profound. I was often brought to tears as I felt the spirit moving in me and felt God's Grace radiating through every fiber of my being. I then began going to Mass every day and was awestruck by how different it was from my earlier experiences. The priest, with his beautiful uplifting homilies, was not a deliverer of wrath, but a direct vessel of God's love. I did my part too, listening attentively and allowing scripture to speak to me. Every day my love for Christ grew deeper, and I was called to make my Holy Confirmation. I will never forget that day or the feeling I had when I was being confirmed in the Holy Spirit. It was like coming home.

At first, I revealed very little about my professional or personal life to the Catholic community, for fear of being shunned. Then, little by little, I began confiding in a select few, and to my surprise, I was not judged, but received as a child of God. I am deeply grateful to God for the close relationships I have formed within the community and the comfort and healing they have brought me.

When we remove the veil and allow Jesus into our hearts, life as we know it is never the same. I believe this to my core. So why do so many people, including myself and many clients, continue to resist Jesus? Is it because we find it difficult to believe that God would incarnate as a human being? God chose to meet us in our human frailty in order to relate to us and save us from ourselves and the illusion of the material world. Jesus is the example and pattern we are to follow. I believe we are here to awaken our own Christ Consciousness, and be the embodiment of love here on earth. We become the embodiment of love when we activate the fruits of the spirit: Love, Joy, Peace, Patience, Kindness, Generosity, Faithfulness, Gentleness, Self-Control, and we Love our neighbor.

Opening myself to Jesus Christ profoundly changed my life. In Christ, I discovered my self-worth, my magnificence in all of my mess. I can feel the Holy Spirit working in me and through me, awakening my Christ Consciousness and integrating all my spiritual healing work. I have become the best version of myself. I know that the strength of Christ is what protects me and provides for me; all I have to do is surrender to God's will and everything unfolds in mystical and magical ways. I am not saying everything is always smooth, but when I am tested and challenged, I know it is Christ who strengthens me. I am finally on solid ground.

"Before I formed you in the womb I knew you, before you were born I set you apart; I appointed you as a prophet to the nations."
~ Jeremiah 1:5

Just as God had a plan for Jeremiah, we can trust and believe that He has plans for us. However, as we get bogged down in the daily grind, it is easy to forget that there is something more out there for us. If you are a fallen-away Catholic I implore you to consider a return to the church and a greater commitment to following Jesus. If you are not Catholic, I ask you to consider exploring a relationship with Jesus through scripture and stillness. This is where the true healing resides; it enables integration of all your own efforts while allowing God to operate through you with unending grace and love that you in turn can extend to others.

Love the Lord your God with all your heart and with all your soul and with all your mind and with all your strength. The second is this: 'Love your neighbor as yourself.' There is no commandment greater than these." ~ Mark 12:30-31

This is what is means to heal through Christ and live wholly, or *holy*. Living Holy means becoming the best versions of ourselves—this is God's dream for us. I have come to realize that my role is to use my spiritual work and my experiences to help others bring down the walls they have erected to keep Him out. When we feel safe to unveil ourselves to the Lord Jesus Christ, we trust that His grace and love is sufficient to heal us.

I have told you this so that you might have peace in me. In the world you will have trouble, but take courage, I have conquered the world. ~ John 16:23

ABOUT THE AUTHOR: Christina Ann Sullivan is passionate about being of service. She feels she has lived many lives within this one lifetime, and that those wide-ranging experiences—including childhood abuse, substance abuse, and dysfunctional relationships—allow her to be compassionate, relatable, and knowledgeable while remaining non-judgmental. Christina is a Denise Linn Certified Soul Coach, Reiki Master, Certified Medicinal Aromatherapist, Spiritual Mentor, Author, and Speaker. She believes her mission is to help her clients access their souls and deepen their relationship with God while exploring a relationship with Jesus through the awakening of their Christ Consciousness and transform their lives on all levels—mind, body, and spirit.

Christina Ann Sullivan
Author, Speaker, Mentor, Catalyst for Christ, Love Agent
Christinaannsullivan.com
Christina@Christinaannsullivan.com

Persevere & Persist
Lisa Sawyer

As I reached the top of a very steep trail in the Great Smokey Mountains National Park, I was overwhelmed by feelings of pride, accomplishment, and joy. I had come so far since my three-week stay at a rehabilitation hospital where I was not allowed out of my wheelchair unsupervised and did not know how I was going to take care of my family.

Three years earlier, I had suffered a debilitating blow to my health. It was the evening of July 3, 2010, and my family was awaiting a fireworks show outside Atlanta. Suddenly, I began to feel a strange sensation in my right arm. Within a couple of hours I could tell my face was drooping, and my right leg felt as if it had a twenty-five-pound weight attached to it. The sight of me sent my husband into a state of concern and as he watched my movements he became convinced a trip to the emergency room was needed. Upon entering the emergency room, the staff treated me as if I was having a stroke and I was given tPA, a drug the doctors referred to as the "ultimate clot-buster". I could not be poked with needles or even get out of bed for twenty-four hours for fear that any puncture of the skin or fall would cause me to bleed to death.

Five days in that hospital and many tests later, I was officially diagnosed with a stroke. The doctors, however, could not determine WHY I would have had a stroke. I was a thirty-eight-year-old, non-smoking, healthy eater who was not overweight. The hospital released me with a walker which I could barely hold, and apparently without anyone even realizing that my condition had gotten worse. I had lost most of the use of my right arm and could only move my right leg forward by swinging it around. My husband spent my first day home caring for me and our two small children—four-and-a-half years and seventeen months old—in addition to making phone calls and scheduling follow-up doctors' appointments and physical therapy.

He called the neurologist we had been referred to but was told there were no openings until August. My husband had explained the situation to the nurse who relayed it to the neurologist, and within an hour we received a phone call back saying he would see me the next day. My story did not make sense to him.

At the office visit, he tested muscle responses, listened to the story about what had happened and then told me he wanted to send me back to the hospital for another MRI. I was reluctant to return to the hospital after having just gotten out, but I instantly trusted this man and felt a connection, so I did as he recommended. Upon exiting the MRI test, this doctor was waiting for me and, already having seen my MRI, said "It wasn't a stroke. It's MS". While a diagnosis of Multiple Sclerosis was devastating, it brought me a small measure of relief. I had been troubled by my "stroke" because I did not know what to do to prevent another from occurring. I did not smoke, drank minimally, did not have high blood pressure or cholesterol, and ate fairly well. So a diagnosis of MS was something I felt I had a chance of controlling.

Once again I was admitted to the hospital where I spent five days undergoing a steroid treatment and my doctor fought to get me into a local rehabilitation hospital instead of the lesser facility where my insurance company wanted me to go. Luckily he made them understand the situation, and I spent another three weeks at the better rehabilitation facility.

The best part about this place was that it did not look like a typical hospital. I did not have to wear a hospital gown or have IVs in my arm and monitors on my body. Still, it was a humbling time with nurses and other staff coming into my room at all hours of the night to check on me. They lurked about, ready to assist with every move I made, sometimes in a kind and helpful way and sometimes in the reprimanding, I-know-better-than-you way. I had to learn to strike a balance between asserting independence and asking for help; arguing with nurses to allow me six hours of uninterrupted sleep, standing my ground on being able to use the bathroom unassisted, and asking for help to put on my bra.

While I am forever grateful to all the therapists at the hospital as well as my in-home therapists and outpatient therapists, I had many instances of feeling overwhelmed or near defeat while in the hospital. I was sent to therapies I just could not do because I had no ability to move any part of my right arm. My breathing was off. Most movements as simple as taking a couple of steps winded me. My speech was affected. Having a conversation was hard. I had to stop every few words to breathe as I could not seem to talk and breathe at the same time. I could not bathe myself in the hospital and was not allowed out of my wheelchair except during therapy. I saw a counselor in the hospital and was in tears every time from an overwhelming sense of gratitude for all the good things that were happening as well as a release of the frustration and sadness I felt from this experience.

I dreaded the weekends because regular therapy did not occur. They had recreational therapy and educational sessions but sitting and listening to all the things that needed to be done to my home to prevent me from falling only made me sadder. Participating in activities with these strangers and waiting for the time to pass instead of being home with my family was devastating. I loved when my husband would bring our kids to see me, but then I would just cry as I held them in my lap on my wheelchair, hugging them with the one arm that I could move. We would go for short walks outside, my husband pushing my wheelchair while my children sat on my lap, but a seventeen-month-old gets restless quickly. One afternoon, my husband left my daughter with me for a couple of hours, and we played cards and watched television. I had to re-evaluate myself and my parenting. I could not let this define me, and I certainly was not about to accept it.

After three long weeks of physical therapy, occupational therapy, speech therapy, and electric shock treatments to stimulate my muscles, my insurance company pulled the plug. I spent the last couple of days at the hospital "practicing" being at home. I had to cook muffins and move around a kitchen, practice getting up off the floor, and going up stairs into a house. I was fitted for a brace for my leg to keep my foot from dropping and practiced walking with my four-footed cane. Then I was released.

As good as it was to leave the hospital and continue my re-covery at home, it was overwhelming and frightening to be at home, without a twenty-four-hour staff to rely on. My husband traveled most weeks for work, and now, after a month at home taking care of the kids, he was due to leave the week after my release. He also had to work on the days leading up to his trip. I was scared to be left alone with my kids. What if something happened and I could not get to them quick enough? I could not drive. I asked a friend to come over with her kids so our kids could play and she could supervise. I asked an out-of-town friend whose kids were grown to stay with us while my husband was out of town.

Daily life was certainly its own type of therapy, and I had a physical therapist and an occupational therapist come to my home to continue to work with me. Once I knew my kids were safe, I felt more comfortable being at home. I reached out to my network and made acupuncture appointments, massage appointments, and chiropractic appointments. I was getting Kangen water from another acquaintance who had been bringing it to me in the rehabilitation hospital. I went to her house regularly to fill up my bottles of the alkaline water. My husband and I researched my diagnosis and what we could change in our lives. I refused to believe I would not make a full recovery. My neurologist loved to share his knowledge, and I was happy to listen and interpret it in a way that had me making a full recovery. I was scared, freaked out, shocked, sad, nervous, hopeful, grateful, and a million other conflicting emotions.

People have asked me if acupuncture works or the water works or if I feel a difference from changing my diet. My answer has been the same every time. I cannot say one of those items worked or did not. All I CAN say is that when I visited my neurologist in February, seven months following my episode, he was astonished at my recovery and said I had already surpassed his expectations. I will never forget those words as long as I live! I had ceased using my cane within a few weeks after I got home and even then it was used primarily when I left the house. By October, I had taken my brace off for good. But I still walked with a limp and had so much farther to go when my doctor told me that. I, in turn, was astonished that he thought this was how I was going to be the rest of my life. It left me emotional anytime I thought about it.

I have a mosaic trivet that I made during recreational therapy one day. Any time I see it in the drawer, I am reminded of this period in my life. I do not have pictures or videos to show or watch, but I have vivid images in my mind's eye and memories which will be with me always. Most people who watched me go through that challenge choose not to remember it or have simply forgotten, since to them I have recovered. People who meet me now are surprised if they find out about this episode. Even to me, it almost feels surreal. I have these images, memories, and feelings about that time, but at the same time, as I go through my daily life, by appearance almost "back to normal", it seems strange that those images and memories were ME. It is as if I watched a rather sad and tragic, yet ultimately uplifting movie.

I am grateful to everyone who played a part in my recovery, ANY part, and ALL parts. As I am writing this piece, I continue to work on my recovery. There are fine motor skills which are still weak, and I try to find exercises to improve them. I can run short distances before my foot drops, and I have to walk, but I cannot skip correctly nor jump on my right leg. I may never get back to the way I was before July 3, 2010, but I am not concerned with going back. At this point in my life, I am only concerned with moving forward.

ABOUT THE AUTHOR: Lisa Sawyer resides in Florida with her husband and two children. She also has three stepsons, a daughter-in-law, and granddaughter. After working in Corporate America for more than ten years, she left to raise her children and pursue at-home business ideas. For the past decade she has been a distributor for Send Out Cards and enjoys getting paid to be nice. She volunteers at her children's school and is an active member of the Jacksonville Chamber of Commerce. She received a BA in Accounting from North Carolina State University and MBA from the University of North Florida and holds her CPA license in Florida.

Lisa A H Sawyer
Author and Entrepreneur
SendOutCards.com/ImagineMore
ImagineMore@comcast.net
904-322-8349

Less Than
Uma Alexandra Beepat

It's funny what we remember from childhood. We could have had the best childhood, yet we tend to focus on certain poignant, turning points that don't fully represent the whole. These memories I like to think of as "soul setting" memories because they charter the waters of life for the next fifty or sixty years.

Though I am not in my fifties, I assume (and heartily so) that I will be in a better place than I am now, and will have worked through the majority of my childhood dreams. Or nightmares. Two sides to the same coin, I suppose.

My deepest memories of my early life can be categorized by two words. Two words that sound simple to the ear but for years created an ache deep inside my heart. They are the words "Less Than."

I have spent the majority of my life feeling Less Than other people. Sometimes it is because people purposely made me feel that way by excluding me, judging me, or not liking me for their own personal reasons. Most of the time, though, it was my own internal monitor creating the Less Than scenario. The other person wasn't even aware of it!

Between people's judgments and my own, my self-esteem got warped. I started to think that whatever I did, it would never be good enough; then, after awhile, that changed to "Why even bother?" I yo-yoed between lying in bed all day, despondent and rejected, and having bursts of energy to complete tasks and for once feel good about myself. Life was a constant struggle.

My earliest memory of feeling Less Than can be traced back to a conversation my mom had with her friend. I remember feeling so proud when she remarked how studious I was, because it was true. Many times she'd passed my bedroom and saw me sitting on my bed, legs splayed out, with all my textbooks on the bed as I studied and studied. As a result of that hard work I got good grades and would be accepted to college. But I didn't hear the pride in my mom's voice about those late-night sessions; what I heard and latched on to for a major part of my life was her last sentence: "She is not naturally bright like her brothers, they don't study and they get good grades, but she has to study all night."

Mom, God bless her, had no ill intent, but heard through the ears of a teenager fighting her own inner struggles, the words were heartbreaking. Looking back, I can see the whole picture. Maybe my brothers did well because they had great memories, or because they crammed for their exams. Or maybe they were naturally brilliant, but guess what? I was too. I chose to study because I was disciplined. I wanted to learn things properly so I wouldn't forget them.

Unfortunately, I didn't get that at the time. I just received the message, "You are not good enough, you are Less Than." So I did what anyone else would do in my situation—I accepted it.

I allowed it to infiltrate my subconscious mind and then I made decisions based off it. I wanted to become a doctor but I thought to myself, *That would be too hard. I am not naturally smart.* I would shy away from challenging tasks and instead chose easy things so I could always shine.

This was only the start of feeling Less Than. The thing is, when a feeling is rooted deep in the subconscious, we then attract similar situations that reinforce that feeling. Of course I know this now, but back then? I could pitch a "poor me" story better than a boy scout could pitch a tent. In fact, I reveled in my "poor me" status.

As a teenager, I was a tomboy. I liked to wear ripped jeans and get on a skateboard. My friends were wearing makeup and noticing boys, but I couldn't be bothered. I was still playing football with them. When I did finally get around to noticing boys, they didn't want anything to do with me. They were going for my friends, the cute girls with the pretty faces and perfume. The girls who unknowingly made me feel Less Than.

Eventually I did start to date and had the unfortunate experience of having a boyfriend, who was emotionally and verbally abusive.

He was also charming and manipulative, one day saying and doing terrible things to me and the next day buying me things and paying me compliments. He wouldn't do these things to a REAL woman, I told myself, he did them to me because I was Less Than. This became a vicious cycle—he would put me down, then I would put myself down for being weak and unable to leave him. The abuse continued for three years before I finally left and even then, I felt like I was a failure for not being able to maintain a stable relationship.

As you can probably imagine by now, this continued for some time. I held the vibration of Less Than, so the Universe kept sending people and situations that allowed me to reenact the victim mentality. When good people crossed my path I pushed them away because I felt I didn't deserve them. Instead, I found people who were suffering with their own demons and hung out with them. I felt safe with their negativity. That was the song I sang for a very long time, and needless to say, it was a hellish life!

The change started with my awareness that I no longer wanted to be this way. I no longer wanted to be negative or depressed or live a life of drama and irrationality. I craved peace and stability within myself, and that craving and awareness propelled me onto a spiritual development path.

I became more aware of yoga and meditation. I had dabbled in these practices throughout my life but now, I completely immersed myself in them. My life needed a reboot!

At this time I was also experiencing symptoms of physical illness. My doctor diagnosed me with Irritable Bowel Syndrome (IBS), and a host of other issues that required surgery. I prayed for a solution that didn't require these extreme measures. I was beginning to understand that these negative emotions within me were beginning to manifest outwardly.

One night, an Indian man visited me in a dream and told me to learn yoga under him. I had no idea who he was, but I felt at complete peace with him. When I woke up I began researching ashrams and yoga programs in India. I had no idea we have ashrams in America too! Then a Google search brought up an ashram called Yogaville in Buckingham, Virginia—just two hours from my home!

As I read through their site, I learned that Yogaville is a spiritual retreat center that offers daily, weekly, or monthly spiritual development classes, including yoga and meditation. They also had a one-month yoga teacher training program. When I saw that the ashram was in honor of Swami Satchidananda, my mouth hung open in surprise. It was the same man who had come to me in my dreams! I immediately signed up for the program.

Each morning we woke up at five-thirty for a meditation and yoga class. Then, after breakfast, we would attend classes and lectures until nine p.m. Living the yogic lifestyle—including a vegetarian diet and a weekly fasting day—really turned things around for me. By the end of the month, my symptoms had disappeared and I felt amazing in my bendy, flexy body!

I also wasn't hanging out with other victims or negative thinkers; I was around people who were serious about creating change in their lives. And you know what? It rubbed off on me. I started to look at the world through a different lens and realized it wasn't the hostile place I had imagined. More importantly, I began to feel like I was Enough; I too had something to offer to the world and it would be a worthy contribution.

Once I returned home, I started my daily meditation and yoga practice while adjusting to the real world. It was rough. Sometimes I still didn't think kindly of myself and I had too many people in my life that were only happy to remind me of what a failure I was. The difference though is I stopped believing them and started believing in myself.

Deep philosophical questions started coming up, and I would debate them within myself. I believe in an Infinite Being of Goodness (God, Source, Universe—they all mean the same to me) and if this Being created me, how could I be bad? Could it be that I wasn't actually "bad," but simply the product of experiences? And if I was the product of experiences, could I then change my course in life by changing my experiences?

I didn't have an answer then, but with faith and a little curiosity, I tried it. And you know what? It worked.

Each day I spent two hours in sadhana (spiritual practice). I would wake up and meditate, do yoga, chant, pull my tarot cards, do self-Reiki, and journal. I refused to leave my room until I had my spiritual body intact! My vibe was lifted. I felt peace within myself and whenever I stepped outside into the world, that peace stayed with me, allowing me space in situations and with people. Space to respond, space to think, and space to expand and contract. It was a beautiful thing.

The peace started to exude outside of me too. I was no longer okay with being classified as Less Than; instead, I found myself sticking up for myself more, letting people know that despite their unhappiness with me, I was happy with myself. I lost friends. And family. But I found freedom. I found myself.

Now, on the precipice of turning forty, I can truly say I am Good Enough. Even better, I am Enough. I have found comfort in my strengths, patience and compassion for my weaknesses, and an overall love of life and everything in it.

I hope my story has moved you. Maybe you have been where I was, or maybe you are still there. It doesn't matter. I did it and you can too. You start by being your biggest cheerleader and then accepting yourself as you are. Being kind with yourself for your faults and weaknesses, and through it all, standing up for yourself. Set boundaries and stick to them.

I can truly say I am happy now. From time to time, the Less Than monster rears its ugly head but I have the tools to meet it head-on. I don't let it fester and then wonder months later why I feel drained or exhausted or unhappy with myself. I am much more forgiving of my behaviors and my habits and I work patiently, ever so patiently, at being better and brighter the next day. I am Enough, and I have no problem letting others know that too.

ABOUT THE AUTHOR: Uma Alexandra Beepat is an author, speaker, healer, and spiritual teacher based in Virginia. She owns Lotus Wellness Center, where she mentors clients in psychic development and other aspects of spirituality. Her book, "Awakened Life," explores her own journey and supports others seeking to create positive change in their lives. Uma is a trained

Psychic Medium from Arthur Findley College in the U.K, as well as a certified Angel Tarot Card Reader, certified Hypnotist, Certified Life Coach, Reiki Master Teacher, and Registered Yoga Teacher. Known as the "Get Real Guru," she is passionate about living authentically and accepting yourself where and as you are.

Uma Alexandra Beepat
Lotus Wellness Center
umalotusflower.com
uma@lotuswellnesscenter.net
facebook.com/umalotusflower

Initiation
Shelley Poovey

"The shamans say that being a medicine man begins by falling into the power of the demons. The one who pulls out of the dark place becomes the medicine man, and the one who stays in it is the sick person. You can take every psychological illness as an initiation. Even the worst things you fall into are an effort of initiation, for you are something which belongs to you"
~ Joan Halifax

It woke me in the middle of the night, like a hungry animal tugging on my leg for food. At first it felt like a dream but as I started to wake more fully the presence remained. I could feel the hatred and rage coming off it as it invited me to rehash my stories of disappointment, abandonment, and failure yet again.

As I sat in my apartment on the edge of Manhattan, staring at this demonic presence, I knew I was supposed to feel intimidated and afraid; that I had brought this on myself for daring to explore this terrain of self-knowledge and self-mastery.

This was just one of many visits from these dark energies over the last few months, and they had made their presence known in very unpleasant ways. By that time, I'd come to the conclusion that they were yet one more source of destructive energy that had been called into my sphere of influence and awareness recently.

I'd been sick off and on for the last year, experiencing strange hallucinations, visions, and disturbing thoughts while battling recurring sinus infections and irregular menstrual cycles. I remember hearing thoughts like, *You're going to be dead soon, then it will be all over* and the terrifying confusion as to where those thoughts were coming from or what they meant. Aside from being the typical overcommitted New Yorker running a busy healing practice, I was generally happy and quite conscious of the life I'd chosen.

My then-boyfriend was so freaked out he went behind my back to seek council from a few friends of mine who were also healers. He was worried I might hurt myself, or something worse.

No one was able to help me. They all assumed I had picked up an entity or was in denial of some deep sickness within me. All I knew was that I felt exhausted on all levels. My own inner guidance system was telling me that I'd taken this journey as far as I could on my own, and that something big was about to shift.

By the time I sat face to face with the angry demon, my relationship had ended and most everyone in my life had distanced themselves from me. They seemed suspicious that a healer could be vulnerable to "bad energy." Though I understood their concerns, I knew I had done my best to follow ethics and guidelines, including shielding myself during my work. Recently, my healing work, and my own personal journey, had taken an evolutionary leap. Were these recent experiences related, or was it mere coincidence?

Darkness

It all began when I attended what I thought would be a lighthearted, fun weekend workshop on energy healing. However, it catalyzed a freefall into deeper realms of mystery, beauty, and magic than I would have thought imaginable. Suddenly I seemed to remember everything and knew that time was an illusion. I could pull information from the universal consciousness and validate it later; I could read people's minds and tell strangers their diseases by touching them or knowing their date of birth. If I knew then what I know now, I might not have decided to take that workshop. But at the same time I am appreciative of the grace and wisdom that has come from it, even on the nights when demons decide to appear.

That demon had chosen to come during a particularly vulnerable time—a few weeks before I was holding my first full-weekend meditation and self-mastery retreat. After years of teaching smaller classes and workshops, it was a significant milestone. As the weekend approached, people expressed enthusiasm for the opportunity, but no one was making the commitment to sign up. This, in addition to my recent hardships, was very difficult to deal with. I felt that it must mean I was a total fraud, probably mentally ill, or worse!

So, after three years of dedicated work on these specific practices, I attempted to give up. I canceled the workshop, and started trying to figure out how to get out of the healing profession once and for all.

That's when I saw a flyer announcing the visit of a Taoist master; he was teaching a practice that sounded very similar to what I'd been working on. The skeptic in me figured I'd go and be proved once and for all what a fraud I'd been, making it that much easier to give it all up and go back to living a "real life" like everyone else.

Instead, I had an incredibly profound experience. First, I discovered that the practice was indeed very much like mine, which confirmed that the knowledge I'd been accessing was coming from universal consciousness. Second, I now had a teacher to help support my own growth and my ability to bring these practices to others. And on the last day of this workshop, during the final meditation, my body felt so strange, and I kept hearing the words, rats, lizards, and snakes. How confusing and terrifying! Were the voices returning? Despite my fear, I continued with the meditation practice as best I could.

That evening I got a call from my father telling me that my grandfather was declining in health and having hallucinations. He had seen rats, lizards, and snakes in his house.

In that moment, I felt a deep connection to my family that was both incredibly satisfying and very uneasy. There was something significant in the clairaudience I was experiencing, but what? I decided for the moment to keep things to myself and see what happened.

A few weeks later, I came down with another mysterious illness. For five days, I couldn't get out of bed. Nothing physical was wrong with me, but I felt heavy and unable to move. I was sleeping a lot as well. When I found out that my grandfather had had a heart attack the same day I fell ill and spent five days in intensive care, I knew something important was happening. I also knew I needed help in figuring it out, so I called a friend and trusted healer.

There, in an eatery on 44th Street and 5th Avenue, we had soup and grilled cheese sandwiches while she consulted with her spirit guides to find out what might be going on.

They told her I had shamanic gifts—specifically the gift of helping lost souls or people in transition find their way to the other side. My grandfather, they added, was coming to me for assistance.

With her help, I was assigned some spirit guides who were there to support me as I worked to ground my energy and help my grandfather in his time of transition. I had always been uncomfortable working with spirit guides, but these came in very benevolent animal forms who seemed to be shielding me from these harsh energies that I had yet to understand or learn to work with properly.

The next few weeks were extremely emotional. My sleep was intense: I was being taught during dream-state. I could feel the spirit guides with me as I woke each morning, fresh with new understanding of what was coming. Thanks to their support, I was also in regular contact with my grandfather.

He made it known how important it was that I attend his funeral, which was devastating in light of the fact that my recent struggles had left me flat broke. Rent was coming due soon, and for the first time since I'd started my healing journey I might not have the money to cover my expenses…yet another indication of my failure. Aren't all healers supposed to be universally supported in abundance? If my grandfather was passing and he needed my help, shouldn't money be flowing in to support us both with ease and grace? Apparently not.

As his passing grew closer, I was spending most of the time crying in despair, confusion, and self-doubt. Was this really my grandfather communicating with me or was I falling deeper into the pits of illusion and insanity?

Light

Two days before his death my grandfather visited me in a meditation and told me not to worry, he would make sure I had the money to attend his funeral, which he confirmed was still very important to him. He told me when he would die and that I needed to be in meditation to help him cross over.

Despite my self-doubt, I agreed, and on the appointed day and time I went into meditation. Sure enough, my grandfather came to me and expressed great fear about crossing over. As I tuned into his energy and the energy around him, a great sense of peace fell over me. I saw the portal to what he would call heaven and felt it was safe for him to cross over.

I then assured him he would be fine and showed him the heavenly gate where the golden light shone through. He smiled, reached out his hand toward what seemed to me to be the hand of God, and took it in his.

That same morning, a handful of long-overdue payments came through. Rent was going to be paid and there was plenty of money for the trip to attend his funeral. Everything started to shift and many of the messages I'd been receiving guidance on started to show up.

An hour later my mother called to say he'd passed peacefully and in the company of his loved ones.

At the funeral, I overheard someone saying that they'd seen my grandfather look up and reach out his hand toward the sky right before he passed. He'd been a beautiful man full of devotion to God, and was able to pass in the way he wanted, full of peace, surrounded by his family. Even though I was not there in body, it was a blessing to be able to be with my grandfather in spirit and assist with his transition.

Afterward, I spent some time at home with my dad, enjoying stories about my grandfather, laughing and celebrating what a sweet and loving man he'd been. Then I began to open up about some of what I'd experienced over the past year—including the disturbing thoughts about what seemed to be about my own death. Though I'd felt isolated, I'd been afraid to open up to them about what was happening, I didn't want them worrying about me.

My father's response deeply surprised me. "Yeah, that sounds like your grandpa. He'd been talking like that all year. He was in a lot of pain and ready to go. It was hard watching him hurt like that."

At that moment, I knew without a doubt that I was fully supported by a force that was much bigger than me, more benevolent than I could imagine, and saw something I was unable to see.

So, the next time I was lying in my bed, staring at a dark, fiery demonic presence, I was not afraid. Instead I chose to let it see me, and in return chose to see it, study it, and know it as deeply as I could. The more I studied it, the more I saw that it was absolutely unreal, like a hologram with no soul or real life-force. It was almost carnival-like in its absurdity, and I knew in that moment that all was well, and that from here it was only going to get better.

All I could feel was pure love, like I was being guided into a space where nothing else could exist, even among the emptiness, grief, self-abandonment, and despair. I realize now that's what lost souls feel, and that in order to help them I must remain anchored to that unconditional love that is omnipresent at all times in order to help them find their way home, into the light.

ABOUT THE AUTHOR: Shelley Poovey is the owner of BodyAttune in New York City, and an expert in manifestation and inner alchemy. Her work explores the relationship between the archetypes of the psyche and the complex neural networks that regulate consciousness in the human body. Shelley offers personal sessions that focus on stimulating our innate capacity to heal and manifest our deepest desires, as well as a monthly subscription-based program that works with manifesting in harmony with the New and Full moon cycles. She also hosts a year-long immersion program around various energy practices. Both programs provide a unique opportunity to engage a balanced relationship between presence, embodiment, and transformation.

Shelley Poovey
BodyAttune
bodyattune.com
Shelley@bodyattune.com
917-362-2827

The Sweet Smell of Transformation
Leah Rubba-Lazarus

My life's journey is not special or unusual. As a matter of fact, I am sure that many of you will be able to relate to different aspects of it. I was a very shy, soft-spoken, and introverted child; this, I suspect, was largely because I did not have siblings for the first eight years of my life. It didn't help that I came from a large extended Italian family filled with many highly extroverted, accomplished, and outspoken individuals. When amongst them as a group I literally felt as though I did not have a voice. My mother was also an extremely vivacious, beautiful, and engaging woman. I always felt as if I lived in her shadow and never met her expectations. As a child, I reacted to these external circumstances as most children do; I took on the belief that I was flawed in some way, that I was never quite good enough. I developed a nervous tic, was diagnosed with a spastic colon, and had a pattern of frequent colds and illnesses at a very early age. I also recall being told that I walked to kindergarten with my shoulders drooped and my head down. One of my saving graces at the time was Rinny, my border collie. Rinny and I were so attached that he literally followed me right into the classroom, and my mother often received a call from the school requesting that she come and pick him up. Rinny helped me feel like I was not so alone.

Despite an underlying feeling of inadequacy, I was fairly popular in high school, which helped me to feel better about myself and gave me a feeling of greater security. Of course, I later realized that our security cannot come from outside of ourselves and that all that we need already lies deep within the core of our Being. That said, being a part of a peer group is an integral task at that stage of development, and I soon found myself listening to the problems of my classmates, whether they were close friends or not, and I became a fierce advocate for the underdog. No matter what a person's behavior was like, I always found the good in them. Later, I would come to understand that we always find what we are looking for. That is how our brain works! These experiences laid the foundation for my future career path as a psychotherapist.

As one might expect, the first two years of college were very difficult for me. I went to a big city university and did not feel as if I fit in or was as smart, pretty, or interesting as the other girls. My old programming was definitely triggered having left the safety and security of my hometown friends. I withdrew for a semester and never felt secure enough to join a sorority. Group situations brought me right back to those extended family dinners where I felt invisible and inadequate. I persevered with my education though and later even went on to obtain two separate master's degrees.

Over the next couple of decades I went through many losses and transitions in my life. It could be easy to view those experiences negatively or perceive them as mistakes; however, I know they were all an essential part of my journey towards greater wholeness and spiritual growth. As is always the way when we are changing old patterns, there were pivotal moments of transformation and moments when I fed the old story of not being good enough. Our conditioned patterns run deep and draw us back, especially during those darker nights of our soul when our ability to cope with the circumstances of our lives is compromised. When I fed those old stories, my life choices reflected it and there were lessons to be learned. When I fed the ones that I desired to believe about myself, I grew in ways I never imagined possible. I truly believe that all of my experiences were a part of my healing journey and served as stepping stones for life as I know it today. What ultimately emerged was a growing awareness that we are all like diamonds in the rough and that the greatest gift we can give ourselves is to learn how to love and accept all of our parts and all of our experiences...the good, the bad, and the ugly. This concept is at the core of what I teach my clients today. It is also what I believe we are here to learn.

Challenging myself to face my fears was another major component of my transition from a shy, introverted child to a more empowered woman, both personally and professionally. One of my pivotal moments was when I had to give my first presentation to the community. At the time, I was the Director of Social Work at a local hospital. For months before the presentation, I told myself that I would be a total failure. Well it is true, we do get what we expect! Even though I had written my speech word for word and was reading it, I lost my place. I remember the dread as I looked out at the audience, totally speechless for what seemed like an eternity. I clearly learned that if we want to change our lives, we need to change our thoughts. So from that moment on, I learned to focus my internal dialogue on what I *did* want and on creating visual images to support my desired outcome. I then stepped into a *feeling* of gratitude in advance of attaining my desire. Connecting to a strong, positive vibration is a crucial part of the manifestation process and helps to promote changes in our brain and old conditioned behavioral patterns.

This manifestation strategy has worked for me in innumerable ways, as I know it has for many of my clients. It was not long before I was able to speak in front of hundreds of people with ease and confidence; I even became a sought after speaker. I manifested the exact home of my dreams, developed a successful private psychotherapy practice, became a team leader in an awesome health and wellness company, and attracted a wonderful husband as well as many supportive and spiritually uplifting friends. There is no doubt that the many blessings I have in my life today are because of this process!

On June 1, 2014, I lived through what was probably the greatest challenge that I have ever faced—the passing of my beloved mother. Being able to support her through the last eight months of her life was an honor that I will cherish always. During that time, our relationship grew deeper and sweeter than ever before. Partly as a result of our heartfelt discussions, she was finally able to open her mind to the possibility that life goes on beyond physical death. It was such a blessing to witness her peaceful acceptance of the next phase of her soul's journey. I never imagined that I would be able to write and calmly deliver her eulogy, but I did. She had become my role model and hero and on that dreaded day, I drew from her courage and strength.

I would continue to rely on that strength to weather several more storms coming my way. Seventeen months after my mother passed, my sweet father made his transition as well. Two months after that, I lost my mother-in-law and one month after that, my closest aunt. Grief is a heart-wrenching experience. It comes in waves and it begs expression. It is akin to leaving a familiar shore, with no idea what your destination will look like. While going through the process, it is essential to let your heart break so that it can mend and you can one day love again. I used a variety of energy psychology techniques and mindfulness to support myself through this difficult time. Whatever feelings begged expression, I welcomed, accepted, and embraced them, knowing they were only a reflection of how well I had loved. During that foggy, middle stage of the grieving process, I felt lost and void of purpose. Yet even in the darkest moments, I held fast to my faith in a brighter new reality. Then, one day, the light broke through, and I could make out the new shore on the other side of grief. It came in the form of a powerful and ground-breaking healing modality called the Aroma Freedom Technique (AFT). I experienced its power and immediately committed to becoming a Level 2 AFT Practitioner and Trainer. Recently, I taught the first in-person certification program in the world and am now on a mission to teach it to as many people as I can. I truly believe it is another way for me to make a difference on this planet, one person, one group, one class at a time.

Through all the ups and downs of my life's journey, my spiritual beliefs have helped me to view my experiences in a way that fosters hope, not despair…peace, not fear. These beliefs have been my guiding light and my source of comfort, meaning, and inspiration. So in closing, I will share a few more of them in the hope that they may be of some value to you as well.

First of all, I believe that at the core of our being, we are all "perfect, whole and complete" physical manifestations of the Divine, and that we come into this world with the task of remembering that one Truth. Consequently, our soul attracts all of the circumstances necessary to learn the lessons that we need to learn in order to remember. We are thus more than the circumstances of our lives and certainly more than the erroneous beliefs we have adopted along the way. By focusing within and learning how to center ourselves in the present moment, we can let go of our mental chatter and begin to connect with the light, love, joy, and peace that lie deep within and is our true nature. I believe that learning how to love and accept ourselves moment to moment and to seek the deeper meaning that arises through the gift of our experiences is ultimately the greatest healing that we can attain.

The following are words I cherish and have been inspired by along the way: *life is unfolding in Divine and perfect order for our best and highest good; it just is what it is; and it is all good!*

Now, at the age of sixty-seven, I can truly say I feel younger, happier, and healthier than ever. As I look back upon my life, I am most grateful for all of the lessons and teachers that have presented themselves, in a multitude of forms, to me along the way. My greatest passion has been sharing the wisdom I obtained from them with others, and I feel so blessed to be able to do so in my life's work and now through the sharing of my story. I hope and pray that it will help to lessen your load and inspire you on your life's journey.

ABOUT THE AUTHOR: Leah Rubba-Lazarus, LCSW, is a holistically-oriented psychotherapist and transformational coach with over 27 years of experience in private practice. Leah integrates a combination of traditional psychotherapy, energy psychology techniques, and mindfulness to facilitate healing and change in her clients. She is certified in Eye Movement Desensitization and Re-Processing, ThetaHealing®, Psych-K, The Emotion Code, and Meridian Tapping and is a certified Level 2 Practitioner and Trainer of the Aroma Freedom Technique. Leah is also a Holy Fire 11 Reiki Master and utilizes therapeutic grade essential oils in her coaching and energy work practice. Leah resides with her husband and two beloved cats in Marlton, NJ.

Leah Rubba-Lazarus, LCSW
Psychotherapist and Transformational Coach
leahrubbalazarus.com
lrlazarus29@gmail.com
856-874-0010

Trust, and All Will be Well

Heather Thomas

Feeling Disconnected

This can't be it, I remember thinking for the umpteenth time on my way home from work. *There has to be more to life.*

It was a beautiful summer day. The air was clear, breeze warm on my skin, and I was coming home with another headache. The car windows were down, I could smell freshly cut grass, hear birds singing and children laughing as they played worry free in the sprinklers. I realized in that moment that I wanted the freedom to create, to live the life I wanted, to lie on the grass, and not have to worry about how I was perceived.

Growing up in a home that emphasized academic success and accomplishment, I gravitated towards scientific and tangible viewpoints. Still, I craved a deeper connection, but having no experience or trust in spirituality I wasn't sure what that looked or felt like. Most of the time I didn't know what I needed to feel happy, and on the rare occasion I did know, voicing it required more strength than I had.

I quickly learned that anything worthwhile was work and the results were often unfair. No matter how hard I tried, I never felt good enough. Every person I encountered seemed so much better than me. I dreamed that one day I could do the things they did with so much confidence, yet nothing I did ever measured up.

Happy, healthy relationships also seemed out of reach. When lonely I looked for companionship in all the wrong places and inevitably ended up feeling empty and used. I'd criticize myself for my poor choice, but the simple truth was that I couldn't allow myself to receive.

Somehow, I got my college degree, found a career, and made myself a life. I found someone to love and trust as best as I could, someone who was stable and safe, who loved and trusted me in return.

I should be happy, I thought as I pulled into the driveway to see my two-year-old son waving at me from the window. *I wish I knew what was missing. I wish I knew where to look.*

Fear and Dis-Ease

It was a stressful summer in the office and there was little room for having fun, being creative, or enjoying my job. I came home with a headache every day. It would start behind my temples, move across my brow, and end up a continuous band two inches wide all the way around. Most days it felt like my head was in a vise.

I'd walk through the door to see joy on my son's face and my heart would break because I was too exhausted to spend time with him. "Not now, sweetie. Mama has a headache," I'd say, then give him a quick hug and retreat into the darkness of my room. My husband usually ended up making dinner and feeding the kids while I rested. Sometimes I made it to the table and sometimes I slept through, missing out on precious moments with our boys. I had no energy or focus for anything.

One night, as I popped a couple preemptive painkillers before bed it occurred to me that I was just covering up symptoms. Something else was happening and needed attention.

"You must have a sinus infection," my doctor said, "Here's a prescription. Take it and let's see if it clears up." For two weeks I felt great, the high-dose anti-inflammatories took away the pain and I could function. Then my prescription ran out and it all came flooding back.

It was October and for the first time I started to feel nervous about my health. I felt a gnawing in my belly and growing heaviness in my chest and shoulders that I didn't recognize. I tried to push it away, but my mind always returned to worst-case scenarios. The doctor ran blood tests and did not seem overly concerned with the results. By this time my headaches had transformed from a tight band to sharp stabbing pains in my forehead, cheekbones, and sinuses. Everything. Hurt. All. The. Time.

I felt tired, lost, hurt, and hopeless. I didn't know where to turn or what to do. I needed painkillers every day and at sixteen double-strength Advil, I still reached for more. I was afraid to leave the house without a bottle of them in my bag.

Christmas came and with it, I got a massive sinus infection. Getting into bed one night, I rolled over to kiss my husband at the same time as he rolled over towards me. We collided and with that, everything changed.

"Fuuuuuuuck! Oh fuck fuck fuck!" I couldn't breathe, all I saw were stars and the pain was so intense I thought I'd be sick. My whole face was on fire, red hot and icy cold needles jabbing, searing their way into my brain. My nose started to bleed again, no longer an unusual occurrence. This time was different. The bump to my nose had been its last straw. Turning on the bathroom light to catch my reflection in the mirror, I felt my heart drop into the pit of my stomach.

"My nose! What happened to my nose?!" Wiping the tears out of my eyes to see better was pointless. My legs wouldn't hold me and I melted to the floor in a pile of tears, mucus, and blood. My nose, so lovely and straight, had collapsed right in the center! The nausea I felt was the result of a thousand nerve endings speaking of the disintegration and collapse of my nasal cartilage. I didn't know what was worse, the pain or the terror of uncertainty.

I continued the vicious cycle of doctor appointments, bloodwork, more appointments, referrals, and more bloodwork, yet there were never any answers. My hope and optimism destroyed. I had nothing left. No faith, no trust, I was dying. I redid my will and personal directive, and took out critical illness and life insurance to set my affairs in order. I wrote a letter to both my boys and my husband in case I died or…in case I needed to die.

Possibility of Hope

In March, at a cousin's funeral, I reconnected with family I hadn't seen in years. It was my Uncle Garth, the Ear, Nose, and Throat surgeon, who pulled me aside and asked how I was feeling. With the threat of tears in my eyes I shared that things weren't going so well. I had just begun to come to terms with my deformed nose, but the pain hadn't gone away. Sneezing was a nightmare, and I was afraid to hold my boys for fear they would accidentally bump my face. There was no spontaneity, no play and certainly no joy in my life.

"Um. I noticed that your nose looks different," said my uncle, "Have you had that looked at?" My eyes welled up and I shook my head. How could I explain to him that I had done all I could and still nobody knew what was happening?

"I've seen this before," he said. "It's called a Saddle-Nose Deformity and there are only a few things that cause it. Don't get scared, but I think you might want to get it checked out."

For the first time, I felt a glimmer of hope. *He had seen this before!* As we were about to part ways, Uncle Garth gave me a recommendation for a doctor and wished me luck.

The Internet is both a wonderful and horrible tool. As soon as I googled "Saddle-Nose Deformity" I understood why my uncle had told me not to worry. There were only four things that caused the condition, all of them frightening. With a bit of hope I landed an appointment with a specialist and showed up to what was an unexpected and horrific nasal biopsy. No warning, no sedation. I was seated in a chair and a man I didn't know came at my tender touch-sensitive nose with long, sharp steel instruments. I braced myself, screwed my eyes shut, held my breath, and pressed as far back into that chair as possible. Afterwards my nose bled for hours.

When the phone rang a few days later, my heart skipped a beat, hope stirred, and I held my breath. "Sorry to tell you, Heather. The results of your biopsy are inconclusive. We don't know for sure what is going on so we've referred you to someone else."

I didn't hear much after that. My family came home to find me with the phone in my hand, a snotty, sobbing mess on the kitchen floor. That night both my boys had stomachaches and for the first time I realized just how much my dis-ease, dis-harmony and fear was affecting the ones I loved. In that moment, something shifted. I took back my power and resolved to find the answers for myself.

Discovery, Reconnection, and Healing

Taking those first uncertain steps towards health, I felt a growing sense of hope. Someone suggested I see a lady who knew about nutrition, alternative healing, and yoga. I did, and it changed everything.

It was mid-June. The warmth of the summer was just beginning and I felt nervous as I stepped into the coolness of that yoga studio.

Physically, I couldn't do very much. My energy was low and the pressure in my face strong, but even so it felt good to move my body and take time to care for myself. It was during relaxation at the end of class that it happened. For the first time in ten months I actually felt better. I felt lighter and my head didn't hurt as much as it had. I could breathe and found a peace I had not known in a long time.

Someone put their hands on my shoulders. It was warm, comforting and I felt seen and supported like never before. "I've got you. It'll be okay. All you have to do is trust. Trust, and all will be well." The touch felt strong and firm, like a warm blanket around my shoulders. It was exactly what I needed. I reached back to place my hand on theirs only to grasp thin air. Confused, I opened my eyes and looked around to see that there wasn't anyone beside me. There was nobody there! At least, nobody that I could see.

Shaken and shocked by what had happened, I nevertheless felt stirrings of possibility for the first time in months. *Trust, and all will be well.* It felt like a door had just been opened.

Slowly, barriers began to come down as I was introduced to things that I had wondered about but had always been afraid to pursue. I started with the more tangible and believable techniques like massage, yoga, and acupuncture, but soon moved on to Reiki and craniosacral therapy, both of which became my go-to whenever I was in pain. A sense of connection beyond the deeper aspects of myself filled my thoughts and as the weeks, months, and years went by my body grew stronger, my perspective widened, and my attitude changed.

As my trust in the Universe grew, I felt better physically, mentally, and emotionally. Likewise, I found that the better I felt, the more I could trust. The words spoken to me during that first yoga class—Trust, and all will be well—had become both my mantra and a self-fulfilling prophecy.

Healthy, Happy, and Living in Harmonious Connection

It has been twelve years since those first headaches began and ten and a half years since I was diagnosed with a serious auto-immune vascular disease called Wegener's Granulomatosis. I no longer have headaches and many of my other health issues have healed or stabilized as well.

There have been more steps forward and backward than I can count. The biggest thing I have learned has been to always get back up again, to accept, forgive, choose differently, and keep trying until something changes.

The message *Trust, and all will be well* has been the foundation for my healing. It took time, but trusting my dis-ease and pain has been a gift. Without those challenges I wouldn't be who I am today. This experience helped me to wake up and transform my life so that I can now do what I do best, and be of service to others on their journey.

My perspective, attitude, and efforts towards self-acceptance and self-care are more important than any test result or diagnosis. I have never felt so confident in my own knowing. It has taken years to get here, to trust in myself and in the Universe supporting me. I now have the confidence and strength to say yes or no according to my own needs. I trust now—and because of that—all is well.

ABOUT THE AUTHOR: Heather is a successful facilitator of health and healing. She approaches life with curiosity, enthusiasm, and love. She enjoys living her yoga, walking her talk, and encouraging others to do the same. As a Reiki master, yoga teacher, and massage therapist specializing in craniosacral therapy, Heather runs a private practice that includes mentoring, workshops, and retreats. An expert in her field, most of Heather's work focuses on helping clients create "Happy, Healthy, and Harmonious (H3) Life Connections." As a long-time resident of Fort McMurray, Alberta, Heather is supported by her family; Russell, Dylan, Ben, and Max the hedgehog.

Heather Thomas, RMT, ERYT
Healthy, Happy & Harmonious Life Connections
heatherthomas.ca
office@heatherthomas.ca
Facebook, Twitter, Instagram: @H3Connections

My Self-Healing Lifestyle
Alexandra Roehr

It is a true blessing to wake up every morning with a sense of love, gratitude, health, and abundance. I feel the essence of life coursing through every cell of my body, and know that today, just like every other day, is another amazing opportunity to continue living my life with purpose and joy.

My life these days is filled with true purpose. I have a career that allows me to be myself; relationships full of mutual respect and a knowing that it is okay to let each other be who they want to be; and a marriage composed of two independent individuals who are fully committed to and honor the divinity of the other. My body feels healthy, balanced, and full of energy and vitality. These blessings flow to me and through me because I live from the perspective that I am a part of something bigger. I am part of Source energy, and therefore I can create a life filled with love that is unconditional and boundless, as all real love must be.

While I never question or worry that I won't feel this way, I do love to reflect on how I got to this point. Awareness, I believe, is the key to freedom. In awareness there is a sense of confidence and true knowing that no matter what happens in life, we always have the ability to realign with the true essence of who we are and create a new reality.

So when I ask, *How did I get here...how did I manifest/co-create this life?* it comes not from a place of doubt but of curiosity. No matter what circumstances I may find myself in, I want to continue living from this perspective, so I can continue evolving, shifting, and healing as a human being and as soul connected to all.

Like the question itself, the answer is deceptively simple. I got where I am because I had the willingness to embrace a Self-Healing Lifestyle, meaning I had the willingness to change any and every aspect of my life that no longer served me or caused me discomfort or dis-ease.

There was a time when life was just OK. I had an OK job, an OK love life, an OK level of health, and OK relationships with my family and friends. For a while, I accepted this. I mean, how could I complain when some people didn't even have a job, had terminal illnesses, or some other awful hardships? Compared to them, I was fortunate. The thing was, I didn't want to settle for just OK. I wanted more. I wanted to have it all and I wanted it to come from a place of love.

I didn't know how to create a life that was more than just OK, but I *did* know it was possible. So every day I would start by simply telling the Universe that I had the *willingness to change*. I had the willingness to do what it took, and I had the willingness to come from a place of unconditional love. Each day I told this to the Universe, and the Universe responded.

I started meditating, which helped me to surrender my ego and trust in the process of life. It also helped me to become very aware of the subtle changes in my life and the opportunities that were being presented to me. I was willing to accept where I was in life, knowing that by showing gratitude I would be allowing the next step to unfold.

I started surrounding myself with people who made me feel good, and stopped judging those that didn't. I started to care about the way I ate and learned what foods made my body healthy. I started to laugh and play. I started to realize that I'd rather be happy than right. I started to be willing to love others for simply being who they are and not who I wanted them to be. I started loving life, and most importantly, I started to be willing to love myself.

There wasn't one specific thing I did to change my life. I simply chose to view the positive in EVERY situation. That part wasn't always easy, but again it came back to the commitment that I had made to be willing to change any and all aspects of my life, including how I viewed the world.

Any time I felt discomfort or dis-ease about something or someone, I would take a step back and ask the Universe to help me understand the bigger picture and view the current situation from a perspective of Divine love. Now, this may seem like an oversimplification, especially when we are faced with something we perceive as "dire," but, really, what was the alternative? Feelings of fear, doubt, worry, anger, regret, and frustration would only keep me mired in my unpleasant circumstances. I knew, because I had lived that way for years and nothing ever changed. I just kept getting more of what I did not want.

For example, there was a point in my life where I was angry all the time. I would get upset over the simplest things or for no reason at all. This anger at times scared me, it made me feel like something was perhaps mentally wrong with me, or it was something that I had to carry/endure for some unknown reason. It then led to the physical manifestations, such as migraines, intestinal infections, insomnia, panic attacks, and fatigue. Back then I did not understand how strongly the emotional, physical, and spiritual body are all connected. I just remember waking up one day and being tired of being tired. I was tired of being angry, sick, depressed, feeling alone, and unworthy. I wanted something more!

So, I began telling myself, *I have nothing to lose, let me just try something new.* And let me tell you, the miracles and healing that started to happen were remarkable.

There were times when the healing would take a few days or even months, but there were also times when the healing would take a matter of minutes—even seconds! The time it took to heal any specific dis-ease or alignment really depended on *my belief* about how fast I could heal that particular alignment. For example, I had decided to start running and one day I injured my foot. I was devastated and so disappointed in myself for not paying more attention in my running. The injury took two months to heal. After I healed, a few months passed and I injured myself in the same way again. Thankfully, I had done more emotional healing by that time and decided to approach the healing differently. I choose not to get upset at myself; instead, I treated myself well, I rested, told myself constantly that everything was okay and that I would heal quickly. This time, the healing took two days! I started to accept that self-love is a very powerful healing tool and chose to apply it to my everyday life.

And all of a sudden, everyday got better and better. My health got better, my relationships got better and my career and finances got better; EVERYTHING just got better.

Having a self-healing lifestyle does not mean I never come across "hard times"; it means I have the tools—balance, love, and joy among them—to handle anything that comes my way. I can always find realignment and healing. All I need to do is have the willingness to surrender to Divine perspective and Divine love.

As I have changed, others around me have changed as well, some without me ever saying a word. Others have come out and asked me how I was able to achieve what I did in such a short period of time. Seeing this transformation in others inspires me to continue doing what I am doing, because what I do for myself I do for the group consciousness as well.

Consider this quote from Gandhi: "We but mirror the world. All the tendencies present in the outer world are to be found in the world of our body. If we could change ourselves, the tendencies in the world would also change. As a man changes his own nature, so does the attitude of the world change towards him. This is the Divine mystery supreme. A wonderful thing it is and the source of our happiness. We need not wait to see what others do."

I believe so deeply in the ability of all of us to heal; it is all a matter of perspective and our willingness to let go of what no longer serves us. In doing so, we develop love, compassion, forgiveness, and acceptance for ourselves and for others. We are all Divine beings who came to this earth to learn, prosper, and enjoy the good health and abundance that is our birthright. All we must do is lay down the ego and remember our connection with the Divine and we can create our own reality. I am living proof.

In fact, I am so sure of this that I have dedicated my life to helping others create their own Self-Healing Lifestyle. In my coaching practice, I hold the energies of hope, possibility, and love so that my clients can develop their own self-awareness and empowerment. We work together so that they can discover and connect with the areas and perspectives in their life they wish to change, heal or shift. Remember, there is no right or wrong way to heal, there is only the willingness to heal!

ABOUT THE AUTHOR: Alexandra Roehr is a Wholistic Life Coach and writer who lives by one simple but profound motto: I love life! I love waking up every day and knowing that anything is possible! She didn't always feel this way. After deciding that she would no longer settle for an "OK" existence, a series of synchronicities led her to the tools and teachers that helped her heal her life. At the heart of this transformation was her willingness to submit to Divine guidance, and today, she assists her clients in developing the tools to heal themselves—Mind Body and Spirit.

Alexandra Roehr
The Self-Healing Lifestyle
theselfhealinglifestyle.com
roehrtosuccess@gmail.com
YOU CAN HEAL!

Mental Health:
The Missing Link
Beth Lynch

As a medium, or one who is sensitive to the thoughts and emotions of those crossed in spirit, I have had the honor of receiving messages for the purpose of assisting and empowering others. These messages are not just academic, but wisdom from a Divine Intelligence that each of us can choose to tap into. In fact, we already hold in the highest consciousness all the answers we will ever need. I have come to know this flow of inspiration will always answer the "why" questions we all have: Why do bad things happen to good people? Why do people do things to harm themselves or others? Why do some people seem to have more happiness, love, and abundance than others? The list goes on and on.

I remember being very young, looking up at the stars and asking God, "Why am I here?" The answer came through meditation and the willingness to listen to my inner voice, or higher power: we are here because we chose to be in the physical expression for the purpose of learning, creating, and healing. Along with others in our "soul group," we share and respond to experiences, choices, and challenges as spiritual beings in a world of matter. My journey has led me to assist people trying to understand and heal their addiction to either illegal drugs and/or prescribed medications.

It all began eighteen years ago. Parents often came to me to connect with a child or young adult who had crossed over, but over time I began to notice that an increasing number of them had lost their son or daughter because of a mental health issue. Clearly, the spirit world wanted us to understand this crisis, and had enlisted me to help.

These clients-in-spirit now come to me on a daily basis to share their stories of depression, anxiety, and even suicide. They also show me the powerful negative effects of anti-anxiety, anti-depressant, and sleep medications on humanity. They refer to these drugs as an "epidemic" that will—and I quote "take down the species before any war."

To understand this, you must understand the effect these drugs are having on the human energy field. We are all hardwired to heal sadness, anger, betrayal, and grief, all of which are "low frequency" emotions. We are also going to experience "high frequency" emotions such as happiness, joy, gratitude, a sense of belonging, and strength. It is part of the human experience, and these drugs interfere with all of it.

I find it mindboggling that modern medicine has not yet learned what Spirit has been sharing with me these many years. Medications continue to be prescribed at an alarming rate, robbing children and teens of their natural ability to cope with feelings of low frequency. All we have to do is turn on the news and we see horrific school shootings and soldiers turning on their loved ones, comrades, and the country they served. It is imperative that we educate ourselves on the side effects of these medications on our emotional and intellectual energy.

We do this by understanding the human energy system, vibration, thought processes, and emotional responses, along with the relationship the personality has with a Higher Power, or Source. This relationship could be traditional (i.e. through religious beliefs) or scientific (i.e. the Law of Attraction), but it boils down to understanding who we truly are—a thinking, feeling and loving species, here to learn how to feel and express emotion.

Even as I write this, I feel the presence of those young people I have channeled. I am their voice and their advocate, and I am here to say that they want to help change things.

I remember one particular family who came to me for answers after the suicide of a young male relative. There's a particular feeling a spirit gives off after an out-of-body suicide, or one that resulted from taking a prescription med or some other kind of substance. The frequency of the body drops so low that the spirit can no longer inhabit it. This is very similar to an out-of-body experience or when the spirit leaves the body during trauma. Many people have reported leaving their body during surgery and hovering above to watch the doctors working on them! Again, this is because the body is brought to a lower frequency by the anesthesia. When I told the family I felt the young man may have died while under the influence of prescription meds, they told me he was not on any medication. This is not uncommon for me to hear, and over the years I have learned to trust myself and what the spirit is telling me. Sure enough, one of family members had cleaned out the deceased's man vehicle and found a prescription medication bottle in the glove box. None of the other family members knew of this, and no one was aware that he had seen a doctor for anxiety. He had only been taking the medication a couple of weeks when he died. At this point, the spirit began to show me pictures of a truck and a gun, and his family members confirmed that he had taken his life in the truck. He also kept showing me the glove box open, his way of saying, yes, the medicine had been in there.

They are just some of the countless mothers and fathers, children, siblings, spouses, grandparents, and friends I have seen in deep pain, grief, and confusion. And I have the gratitude and relief they experience when they learn what happened in the final moment of their loved one's life, especially when they get the answer to as why that person took their own life.

These readings bring great comfort to the spirit as well. He or she gets the chance to tell their loved ones that they were not acting of sound mind, but had been struggling with mental illness. But there is a larger message here. Somewhere along the line we have forgotten our connection to Source, and this imagined separation leads us to create very challenging circumstances, personally and on a global level. We have only to look around our planet to see the evidence of this.

When the session begins I get a vision of a Picasso painting, with the profile of a face distorted. Then I see the flatline, like we see on the hospital monitor when someone passes away. It is in that flash I know I am connected with one who feels responsible for taking their life. The Picasso symbolism is the altered perception of their life. This is how they express the disorientation and the inability to rationalize. This is where the Self and Spirit completely detach. In metaphysics the Self and Spirit need to be working together. The Spirit or Consciousness knows this is one reason it has returned to physical form. This concept may seem unnatural and confusing, but it is the truth.

The flatline symbolizes a person who is merely existing in the world, due to low frequency. This occurs through undisciplined thought patterns (which creates reactive emotional expression instead of active or disciplined) that in turn leads to an unhappy perception of life, unhealthy lifestyles, depression, anxiousness, and increased addictive behavior. Think about this for a moment. When you only "exist" in a relationship, job, or experience it can be unfulfilling and even depressing if you do not move the self through or from the experience. You are void of emotions of higher frequency, which are happiness, fulfillment, and joy. Remember, we are here to be creative and loving beings. To be "functioning" at our Divine potential is why we come here. To evolve.

When one (Self) makes the choice to take their physical life they are in complete separation with their Spirit. They show it much like an out-of-body experience; they are observing the act in which physical death is the outcome.

The epidemic of over-prescribed medications is keeping society away from feeling the emotions necessary to heal. According to spirit, just *two percent* of people (including children) benefit from medications. That's because the majority of these medications are of a lower frequency than our natural frequency. That's when I see the flatline.

In one case, a young girl filled with love and God kept showing me a tiny orange pill. Her mother said she was not on any medications and the toxicology report backed that up. Yet she was showing that little pill. It was confusing but I cannot change what I am shown. I unconditionally trust these visions and am extremely careful in interpreting them. But the question remained, "Why would she take her life?" She had a very close relationship with her mother and her sister, wouldn't at least one of them noticed her confusion or despair?

Shortly after, I was having a completely unrelated discussion with another woman, when she mentioned the odd reaction she had to her birth control pills. As she said this, the young girl I had channeled literally flashed into my vision. She was there to show me the little orange pill! I contacted her mother immediately and asked if she was on birth control pills, and she confirmed that she was. Not many women taking birth control pills will get to the point of a Spirit/Self separation, which only made the specificity of this reading more profound. Even after all these years, Spirit never fails to amaze me.

I only hope that the information gained through my readings can help a doctor, mother, father, or sibling recognize the warning signs for someone they love or are treating. Science and spirituality can work together—indeed, they are meant to—and while the relationship between the two has come a long way, it is not far enough. If it were, meditation—not medication—would be the prescription for stress. In my channeling sessions I have seen miracles and I have seen the depths of sadness. Let us honor these messages and learn from them.

When I asked Spirit why the world is the way it is, their answer was, "You have evolved technically as a species, but not spiritually, and you are living the consequences. It is not a punishment but a consequence. That is what earth is for…"

There is no greater evidence of this consequence than the self-harm we do to our bodies and our spirits. We can no longer afford to pretend we are separate from Source, or continue to deny our natural abilities to heal and raise our own frequencies. The next time a doctor prescribes medicine for you or someone you love, don't just blindly take it. Use your spiritual discernment to ask yourself—what is the true source of my problem and is there another way I can solve it? The inescapable truth is that we are both human and spiritual beings—and we must embrace, nurture, and create from this truth.

ABOUT THE AUTHOR: Beth Lynch is an Intuitive Consultant,

Medium and founder of Inner Light Teachings based in Upstate New York. For more than twenty years she has helped her clients heal by connecting them to loved ones who have crossed over. Lynch is especially passionate about helping those who have lost family and friends to suicide and other mental health issues. She also volunteers to educate people of all ages about the power of meditation and devotion to higher awareness. Beth Lynch is a graduate of Delphi University's Patricia Hayes School of Metaphysics and the Arthur Ford School of Mediumship.

Beth Lynch
Medium / Meditation Teacher / Intuitive Consultant
innerlightteaching.com
info@innerlightteaching.com
888-271-4487

From Trauma to Transformation
A Journey of Self-Healing from Childhood Sexual Assault
Melanie Noullett

Once upon a time there was a little girl that loved to play outside and with friends. She had a sweet smile, freckles upon her face, and a sparkle in her eye. She loved her family and she loved her pets. All innocence and trust, she loved roaming the neighborhood on her green bicycle with the banana seat. Then one day, that innocence was lost to a stranger. The little girl raced home to her brother. He did what he could to comfort her but they were both afraid. There were parents, police, questions, and ID line-ups, but nothing, not even a little tape or glue, to fix that little girl's heart. Her family had never learned to ask for help. They didn't even know that they could. Their innocence had been lost as well, and though there would be many more good times, love, and laughter, it would take decades for them to heal.

That girl did well in school, had lots of friends, and was usually pretty happy on the outside. But inside she doubted herself, she never thought she was good enough and she was often scared: scared of the dark, scared of being alone, and scared of not being loved. She became an athlete and loved the snow, crisp air, and freedom on the ski hill. Skiing was her passion, but she didn't have the strength or courage it took to keep going when she wasn't the best. So she moved on to things where she could more easily obtain perfection. She worked hard at university and boosted her self-esteem with high grades, scholarships, and high achievement.

She married a loving, supportive man who gave her the unconditional love she craved. Marriage was good; they loved, laughed, and danced together. He worked, she studied and they believed in each other and their love. Then they were blessed with three beautiful children. Their love for each other and their children was so strong but they still faced many challenges...

challenges that led her on a journey to freedom and truth.

The Road to Healing

Whenever you experience feelings that you don't understand, chances are you can find the answers in your past. My experiences have shown me that there are deep layers in our subconscious and unresolved trauma has a way of seeping into our current reality and often wreaking havoc until we finally open ourselves up to healing. It took psychosis to finally get my attention, but looking back I can see there were more subtle warning signs in the anger I felt and was afraid to express.

The birth of my second child, while joyful, began a period of emotional instability for me. There was a lot of stress with her birth and the health problems that she experienced afterwards. I started to feel more extreme emotions and experience ups and downs. I remember one day I was nursing my new baby. I desperately wanted her to fall asleep so I could spend time with my four-year-old son, but he kept interrupting us and making noise that kept the baby awake. I remember feeling such anger towards this little boy that it scared me. Later, as the children grew it was their fighting with each other that triggered anger. This anger would eventually lead me to seek out alternate healing methods.

I didn't know what to expect when I walked into the thought field therapy demonstration at the local university—all I knew was that I kept hearing about it and my intuition was telling me to check it out. I was pregnant with my third child at the time, and although I was only about five months along it felt more like full-term. Needless to say, sitting in the lecture theatre chairs was extremely uncomfortable. I focused on this discomfort as I tapped along on different acupuncture points, and about twenty to thirty minutes later, I suddenly realized that my discomfort had completely disappeared. I actually felt as if I wasn't pregnant at all! The presenter explained that this was how the therapy works: you hold the feelings of pain, discomfort, anger, grief, fear, et cetera in the thought field as you tap on a specified sequence of acupressure points, and somehow, the feeling is dissolved.

Completely amazed, I volunteered to be part of the next demonstration. This time, instead of tapping along with the group,

I was brought to the front and asked about the problem I was having. I talked about how angry my kids were making me and, rated that anger a 10 on a scale of 0 to 10 when I imagined them fighting and disrupting the presentation. I was then asked to tap through a few sequences of acupressure points and in less than five minutes my feelings of anger had completely dissipated. Even more astounding was that for weeks after their fights no longer triggered me. I had several subsequent sessions with the practitioner and seemed to be processing all kinds of emotions that were locked away in my body. Things would come up and with tapping they would dissipate.

The next step on my healing journey was Reiki. I had picked up a pamphlet about a Reiki class for couples and wondered if it would help with the delivery of our third child. My husband and I attended the Level 1 course and both had a profound experience. As the practitioner gave me Reiki, I felt paralyzed in a bubble of intense energy that completely overwhelmed me and seemed to be radiating throughout my body. I didn't know what it was, but it felt like a miracle.

This was when my healing journey became a spiritual quest. I felt the higher power that connects us all and although I didn't understand it I knew without any doubt that it exists. Around this time, I also read a book called "Loving What Is" by Byron Katie and it truly transformed me. In fact, it was the first time in my thirty-five years that I remembered feeling complete peace. Prior to reading that book I had been searching for answers. I loved being a mother, but my children triggered emotions I didn't understand. Byron Katie taught me to instead live in the question and to fully investigate what was true. I began to realize that my problems with my children stemmed from beliefs that did not reflect the truth of my current reality. And as my perspective changed, so did the world. For a period of several weeks, I was smiling and laughing in a different way, and I could see beauty in everything. I had truly found inner peace. But the transformation was not complete. There was still much work that I needed to do to fully heal.

Psychosis or Spiritual Awakening

There is a downside to experiencing complete peace and that is you want to feel that way all the time. It is almost like the high someone gets on drugs. My "fix" was self-help books. What I didn't understand was that deep inside, something was missing. I was always achieving, yet I still struggled with self-love and acceptance. After years of waiting for me to deal with the past, my body finally decided it was time to give me a wake-up call.

A few months after being "enlightened" by Katie's book. I experienced what the doctors called a post-partum psychosis. It was the oddest thing—I felt so full of love and forgiveness and was able to truly be authentic when talking with people. However, I also began to communicate with my deceased cousin, which confused my very logical and scientific mind. I developed a myriad of very strong fears; for example, I took my children to the doctor because I was worried about environmental toxins. I vacillated between clarity and confusion. My body seemed to move on its own and I felt a need to pray although I was not sure whether a miracle was imminent, or a disaster. I ended up on the psych ward of the local hospital.

As awful as this may sound, it was actually harder on my family than it was on me. I felt like I was meant to be there, that it was an opportunity to learn and help others. The other patients all seemed to represent someone I loved and every conversation seemed to help me grow. While there were certainly some confusing and scary aspects of the experience, I always could see the silver lining. My knowledge of thought field therapy, Reiki, and the work of Byron Katie all helped me to handle my present circumstance in a positive and uplifting way. Now that the experience is over, I know that I was able to shed a lot of faulty beliefs that had been part of my subconscious, especially around religion. I had developed a new connection to Creator that was very different from my religious upbringing and that was okay. I was truly awakened spiritually.

The most important thing that came from the hospitalization was that I was able to talk to my family members about the sexual assault that had not been mentioned in over thirty years. The event had surfaced with the psychosis, and I feel deeply that it was the underlying cause. I also believe it was no coincidence that this transformative period occurred when my oldest child was the same age I'd been at the time of the assault.

Discovering the Angels

After being released from the hospital, I began to experience amazing synchronicities. I found miracles and symbolic meaning in everyday things, and I felt like I had a profound understanding about everything in my life. When I took time to be mindful I was able to tune into my inner self and the guidance of Creator. I also started to witness the work of angels. I discovered angel cards and with the help of their daily messages I learned to follow my heart and share my story of transformation. Much of this sharing came in the form of music. I had never been creative before, but now I found myself writing and singing songs. Each had a chorus that expressed how I wanted to live my life.

Letting go of judgement, letting go of expectation
Living in the moment I learn to love myself

Letting go of fear, letting go of anger
Listening to my heart I begin to live my truth

When we pay attention and our hearts begin to wake
We will be guided to our destiny and evolution will take place

My songs allowed me to open up and become vulnerable, releasing the pain and heartache hiding inside. The words began to work magic and create the life that I truly wanted. I was literally singing my way to healing.

Crazy or Connected

Whenever I think I have things figured out life throws another challenge at me. Since my initial transformation I have had two more peak experiences—both of them in the autumn—when my connection to All That Is overwhelms me. Each time I experienced a manic episode, when my creativity overflowed and my understanding of mystical ideas and connection to my psychic senses deepened. The trauma of the past and unexplained emotions also bubbled forth and I was once again able to remember events with more clarity. Though I have no official diagnosis, I know there is some unexplained connection between my spiritual development, the trauma of my past, and my mental health.

During these periods of heightened awareness, I have seen the face of a wise sage in the mirror that speaks through me and talks about the earth and her wisdom. I have sat on the riverbank with an eagle, remembering the experiences and feelings of an old shaman and chanting in an unknown language. Am I crazy or connected? I choose connected, and though I take low doses of medication, I live a normal life, taking care of my family and helping others through their own transformation. I have been guided to true forgiveness and more than anything I trust the journey that I am on.

When you remember love and act from your heart
You release the pain and the memories you've caused
It is never too late to make up for the past
Feel love and forgiveness given to you
When you open your heart and choose to live true

ABOUT THE AUTHOR: Melanie is the founder of Tiger Lily Transformations. She provides energetic healing and intuitive peer guidance to people choosing to transform their lives and those experiencing a spiritual awakening. Melanie holds a Master's degree in Environmental Science and began studying alternative healing methods in 2009. She is an avid reader and seminar enthusiast, integrating what she learns into her work. Melanie also has a passion to share her own personal story through song writing. She is developing her gift further by writing songs that incorporate other's stories to inspire individuals on their own journey of transformation.

Melanie Noullett
Tiger Lily Transformations
findclarity.com
tigerlilytransformations@gmail.com
250-613-8758

Intuition + Visualization = Divine Restoration

Amber Shannon

Back in 2006, I was living the ideal life, at least the one prescribed by society's standards. I had everything I was "supposed" to have—a college degree, a spouse, a home, and a stable job—yet I wasn't truly happy with any of them. For example, my job at the time was medical billing, which paid the bills, but stifled my soul. I felt like an automaton, a robot, mindlessly processing medical claims day after day. One of the things I dreaded most was having to bill people with no insurance and who I knew couldn't afford to pay, while at the same time seeing the insurance companies getting a steep discount or denying a claim altogether. The injustice of it broke my heart and gave me a sick feeling in my stomach.

I was also suffering from debilitating migraines at the time. They were so painful that I would have to stop whatever I was doing, close all the blinds, and lay down in bed for hours. I took over-the-counter pain medicine so frequently that it eventually stopped working and I had to start seeing a neurologist. The prescription medication worked amazingly well, but I never felt comfortable taking it. I was scared of the possible side effects, and knew that I didn't want to be on it for the rest of my life, but it seemed I didn't have a choice.

Day after day, I woke up feeling miserable and disconnected from life. I didn't want to get out of bed, and there was a constant feeling of emptiness and unfulfillment within me. I was simply existing, and often in a state of suffering, either physically or emotionally.

One day, I finally reached my limit. I couldn't bear living like that anymore—pretending to be happy, suffering physically, and settling for mediocrity. I was sick and tired of being sick and tired. I decided that if I was going to live, I was going to live fully. A conviction rose up from within me saying, "There HAS to be more to life! This can't be all that there is!" I began fervently asking God for guidance on what I should do; how I could change my life. Then, one day, while on a break outside at work, something happened that would change the course of my life forever. It was a sunny day, and I was sitting by the canal, feeding the ducks and turtles, when I heard a voice say to me very clearly, "You are in the wrong life." This voice was not outside of me, it was inside of me, yet it wasn't my own voice. I was startled at first, but somehow knew this answer was in response to my requests for guidance and direction. After pausing a moment to take in what just happened, I said, "Okay. If I'm in the wrong life, show me the right one."

In the days and weeks that followed, I was led to one resource after another in the form of teachers, authors, books, and even television programs. One afternoon, while doing exercises from Louise Hay's book, "You Can Heal Your Life," I had a profound revelation. My migraines were caused by the pressure I put on myself to please other people! I was creating the life I thought they wanted me to have! Then I saw a vision in my head of me "painting my life" on a canvas in an elaborate gold frame and showing it to other people (It would be the first of many "clairvoyant metaphors" I'd receive). With just this one simple revelation, the migraines began to lessen.

Around this same time, my boss asked me to cover the office while he was away on vacation. Shortly before he was to leave, I started feeling like I was getting a sore throat. In a panic, I ran to the doctor. There was no one else to cover for me, and I feared that if I was out sick, my boss would have to cancel his vacation. The doctor gave me an antibiotic that I had never taken before. I thought nothing of it though. I completely trusted him and took the antibiotics as prescribed.

About a week later, I was visiting my family in Sebastian, Florida—a couple of hours north of Fort Lauderdale, where I resided. All of a sudden, I started having digestive problems.

Thinking it was something I ate, I took some over-the-counter medication, but the symptoms got progressively worse. I woke up in the middle of the night with excruciating abdominal pain. Eventually it passed, only to return in waves an hour or so later. This continued throughout the night, and I prayed to God and my angels for help. During one of my reprieves, I got on the computer, desperately searching for what could be happening to me. At first, nothing seemed to fit, then I came across a bacterial infection, Clostridium Difficile, or "C. Diff." Immediately, I *knew* that was it. All the articles said it was rare for someone my age (I was twenty-eight at the time) and usually occurred only after being in the hospital (which I had not), but it did not matter. It was one of the strongest intuitive feelings I've ever had.

As I read further, I learned that C. Diff can live in the system without overpopulating and causing damage if it is kept in-check by other healthy bacteria. The antibiotics I had taken not only wiped out any bad bacteria in my system, but all of my good bacteria as well, creating the perfect environment for the C. Diff to take over. It was a very serious condition that could lead to a hole in the intestines, which could be fatal if not treated right away.

Immediately, my grandmother rushed me to the emergency room. Though I had never been in the hospital before, I was in too much pain to be nervous. After explaining my symptoms and getting my blood drawn, I pleaded with the doctor to test me for C. Diff, but he refused because I did not fit the normal parameters. Instead he ordered x-rays and an abdominal scan to rule out any other possible causes. As I laid on the table in the cold, dim room, preparing for the abdominal scan, I began talking to my angels in my mind. This was a something I just recently started practicing after reading and listening to the works of Doreen Virtue. As I tuned into them, I could feel their presence all around me. In my mind's eye, I could especially see two very large angels hovering over me, one on my left, and one my right. They looked like big, sparkling gold, transparent figures. A wave of peace washed over me, and I knew it was them, comforting me.

After the abdominal scan, I was brought to a private room to wait for my results. The waves of excruciating pain continued, getting worse each time. Once again, I pleaded with the doctor to test me for C. Diff, and this time he agreed. As I laid down to await the results, I closed my eyes and started praying to my angels again. This time, I not only sensed their presence, I felt the hospital bed begin to move! It felt like people were gently rocking the bed from left to right, the way you might comfort and rock a baby. Then, a warm, loving sensation began to flow all around and within me. A few moments later, my mom came back into the room, as well as the doctor, who told me what I already knew—it was C. Diff.

The doctor gave me a prescription for another antibiotic, and advised me to follow up with a gastroenterologist once I got back home. About a week later, I visited with a doctor that was recommended to me by a friend. He was one of the top gastroenterologists in the area and had a very good reputation. During my consultation, however, he gave me a bleak prognosis, saying that I would probably never have normal, healthy digestion ever again. I absolutely refused to accept that, and left his office bound and determined to be completely healed, no matter what it took.

Once I got home, I continued to take the antibiotic I was prescribed. I also began looking up holistic remedies for digestive health and practicing creative visualization, which I had been learning from Shakti Gawain's book of the same name. After a month or so, my digestion was completely healed. Now, I'm sure the medication and holistic remedies played a part, but I truly believe creative visualization is what brought my healing into full manifestation. I practiced it at least three times a day, and would invoke such strong emotion that I would be crying tears of joy and gratitude for my total and complete healing. In fact, it worked so well that I began practicing it for other things, including clearing up my acne-ridden skin. At that point, I had been suffering from moderate to severe acne for more than fourteen years, with off-and-on success from traditional dermatological treatments. Without changing anything else in my skin care routine, I completely cleared and healed my skin within three weeks by practicing creative visualization. I did it in the same way—three times a day, visualizing my skin smooth as a baby's, again to the point of crying with gratitude.

Over the years, I continued practicing these techniques and studying everything I could on the topics of spirituality and personal growth and development. I have had numerous "Aha!" moments and experiences of divine revelation, specifically through meditation. These experiences opened my eyes to the reality of our true essence as spiritual beings who are temporarily inhabiting physical bodies. I have also learned firsthand the powerful role our thoughts play in affecting our physical world, and that our bodies are our best friends. They are the keepers of our soul, and will speak to us whenever something is out of alignment with our divine life path and not for our highest good. I now know that when my body starts speaking to me through symptoms, it means I have ignored something too long. I have since developed the habit of checking in with my body frequently throughout the day, and I also practice a few other techniques to keep the communication flowing.

Although those experiences from years ago were scary, they taught me some of the biggest lessons of my life. I absolutely would not be who I am today without them. It was like I called out to God and the Universe for help, and they said, "Okay, you want the truth? You've got to get rid of this, and this, and that…because those things that are not for your highest good are taking up space in your life, and the goodness you desire cannot flow in until they are gone." When I look back at that life, it is virtually unrecognizable from the way I live today. I'll be honest, some of the changes I had to make were extremely difficult; however, they were also the most important. Not only did I do what I needed to heal my body, I also let go of that unfulfilling job and left an eight-year relationship that I knew from day one wasn't right for me. Since then, I say with tremendous gratitude, my digestion is healthy, my skin has stayed clear, and migraines are no longer a part of my life.

When one's life is transformed as mine was, it is impossible not to want to share it with others. My work as an Intuitive Development Coach has enriched my life in ways that only being of service can. As a strong believer that we all have the innate ability to heal and connect with the divine, I assist my clients with mastering the art of intuitive development to create the health, finances, and relationships we all truly desire.

ABOUT THE AUTHOR: Amber Shannon has been working in the field of intuition since 2008, serving as a channel for divine communication in which she facilitates her clients' transformation. Amber's work is rooted in the understanding that when the flow of energy between the heart and the mind is strong and congruent, people behave in loving, rational ways; they are also able to tap into their "inner GPS" and use it to navigate life's twists and turns and create rich, fulfilling lives. Amber's mission is to assist with the elevation of planetary consciousness by helping people all over the world to re-establish this heart-mind connection.

Amber Shannon
Intuitive Development Coach
Amberlina.com
Amber@Amberlina.com
213-444-3137

The Solution is in the Problem
Kathy Sipple

"Sitting at our back doorsteps, all we need to live a good life lies about us. Sun, wind, people, buildings, stones, sea, birds and plants surround us. Cooperation with all these things brings harmony, opposition to them brings disaster and chaos." ~ Bill Mollison, Introduction to Permaculture

The Problem

I am a Reiki Master who is also an entrepreneur. I work mostly from home as a social media marketing consultant. I value the ability to pop outside to poke around in my garden between client appointments (online, so my grass-stained knees don't bother them a bit.) My backyard is my little slice of paradise where I apply my permaculture design lessons I am learning as I study for a permaculture design certification. Permaculture is a portmanteau for permanent + agriculture, or now, more accepted simply "culture." When I take time to observe them, plants are among my wisest teachers.

Ramps, mushrooms, and other plants are thriving happily in the hugelkultur bed I constructed. Hugelkultur means "hill culture" in German and is a type of permaculture-raised bed that mimics the conditions found in the rich soil of the forest where fallen trees decay in place and create rich humus. In my garden I have buried rotting logs at the base to supply a slow release of carbon. It is built quite a bit higher than most raised beds; therefore, maximizing available planting space into the "hill" sides and increasing potential yields in a small space.

My husband and I removed much of the turf grass in our backyard, preferring wood chips to cut down on watering needs and to help build soil. I had a plan for that sod—it went on top of the hugelkultur bed, grass side down, and topped with a layer of compost. Putting the thing together was a lot of work and the yard looked a chaotic mess as I dragged rotting logs, bunches of twigs, fallen leaves—even the Christmas tree I held onto rather than dragging it to the curb—and finally the plants, mostly perennial fruits and vegetables. Once the pieces were assembled, in a way that made sense, the result was a masterpiece, at least to me—a garden that produces each year with little effort on my part.

One afternoon, as I pluck some asparagus for dinner, I consider the current state of my business: 1) the corporate consulting work I'm doing is lucrative, though usually sporadic, short term, and often unfulfilling; 2) I often don't feel aligned to my client's success; 3) trading time for dollars feels limiting; 4) I'm very passionate about my community environmental and permaculture activities, but my contacts in that area don't appear to have a budget to hire me; and 5) I miss my work as a healer, which I practiced back in Chicago but have not been involved with since moving to Indiana. The challenge? How to integrate these seemingly disparate interests and skills into a new business model. "How," I ask myself, "can I translate my interest in green living into the other kind of green—money!?!" It's time to do an energy audit on my business!

Using My Edge

In permaculture the edge is a special place so I begin my audit there. The edge effect describes an ecological phenomenon that happens where two habitat types come into contact, and refers to the opportunities created when these two types use their natural properties for the best effect, resulting in greater diversity. The edges are the interfaces of ecosystems, integrating them together, allowing them to share and cycle resources. This creates more useful connections, acting as a net and sieve for energy that captures and contains more useful elements between systems. We can emulate these natural patterns to bring systems back to life more rapidly.

What overlap existed between my two ecosystems, business, and environmentalism? Where was my edge? Well, people who care about the environment often need to send emails, create online petitions, launch crowdfunding campaigns, build websites, and use social media, right? My hypothesis was that they did not have money to pay for me to consult with them, but how else could I make the system work?

Starting Small

Another permaculture principle suggests starting small and building on success, with variations. Another is making the least change for the greatest effect. I begin to look for the leverage points in my system and decide to host a free online workshop series called "Social Media for Environmentalists" and invite all my environmentalist connections via email and social media.

I already have the material for all of the lessons I present; it's just a matter of contextualizing the workshop for this niche audience, which is easy and fun for me since it's my passion. I already own a license that allows me to host these workshops so there is no extra cost there. The only input is my time, which I have already been giving as a volunteer anyway.

At the end of the series, I get many thank yous and requests to make the series available through recordings so the information can be reviewed and shared later. I propose that one of the attendees volunteer to process, edit, and upload the video; otherwise, I will do so if a certain financial contribution level is attained collectively. Small and large donations come from several sources and the amount is quickly raised.

I host a number of other workshops in like manner and find myself enjoying my work more than I have in a long time. Instead of working one-to-one, shifting the paradigm to one-to-many makes it possible for me to share my gifts with more people and help them to effect more change. The recorded video builds a legacy that allows the gift to be shared into the future as well.

Synthesis

"We look at flows between things—flows of water, energy, nutrients, information. Every time we link things together, we create more abundance than when they are separated." ~ Starhawk

A new challenge arises when I get a call from Randall, a friend I met through my environmental work. "Hi, Kathy. I've written a booklet, Permaculture Solutions to Climate Change, and I'd like to get an estimate from you to put a website together for me. I want to promote the book so I can give away free copies to schools and others who will put the information to good use. I thought of you first since I know you care about this topic."

Randall has gotten an eco-responsible printer; the cost is about four times what I would normally charge to build a simple website. *This makes no sense*, is my first thought. He's going to pay thousands of dollars for the book and then pay me on top of that, all to give away a book for free? How's that going to work? I decide to keep an open mind and apply a permaculture mindset to this request. I tell him I need some time to think about it. Another permaculture principle: *Observation is the most important step. Take time to assess the resources nature has handed you and then look for solutions that work with the least amount of effort.*

Over the next day or two I have time to consider possible solutions.

I already built a website in support of the environmental podcast I host. Why not interview Randall on my podcast and create a page about his project and the interview rather than building him his own website? That would certainly require less work and the content would reflect well on my own project too; Randall would benefit from the awareness and web traffic already in flux with my site, versus starting from scratch.

There is also the cost of the book to consider. I suggest that we create a crowdfunding campaign to let supporters help him with printing and distribution costs, as well as any additional marketing services I wanted to offer him to support his effort. He could still give away an eBook version of the book for free to make sure price was not a barrier.

Randall agrees, and I set about the familiar steps of launching a marketing campaign.

This project immediately feels different than any other I've done in the past. I'm not looking at the clock and trying to decide what is billable and what I will do on my own time. Our fates are intertwined and I think only of how to make the project successful.

One thing I notice is this client asks fewer questions of me about my strategy or "Why do I need to do this or that?" Because we are united in this effort, he trusts that whatever I suggest is for our highest and best good.

Within a few weeks everything is in place and we are ready to launch the campaign. It's an all-or-nothing situation—if we don't raise 100% of the funds needed, all pledged funds are returned to donors. Plenty of folks opt for the free download—in fact, people in dozens of countries across the globe, in places as diverse as Ghana, Greece, India…Just three weeks into the project we hit the goal amount to cover the costs of printing and distributing the book!

Randall happily pays me my marketing fee from the amount collected and tells me, "You really take a permaculture approach to marketing. I didn't expect that!"

I glow, knowing I'm starting to find my way back to a healthy, happy, sustainable business.

"Observe Nature thoughtfully rather than labour thoughtlessly"
~ Masanobu Fukuoka 'The One Straw Revolution'

One permaculture teacher advised that the best tools in your design kit are a hammock and time. Time to just observe the flow of energy that is already flowing through the system and working with the landscape rather than against it.

As an entrepreneur, it's sometimes hard to see our own energy patterns since we are so immersed in the day-to-day operations. In my individual marketing consulting practice, I now offer "energy audits" to other entrepreneurs to help them find their own edge where they can create new opportunities and work smarter, not harder.

In early 2015 I also launched a membership site called CoThrive where small businesses can learn the same principles affordably and sustainably, over time, by working with one another in a fun and interactive learning environment. The group has attracted many non-traditional marketers such as farmers, healers, coaches, writers, artists, and musicians who wanted (or needed) to master new media skills, and who also valued co-creation and interconnectedness.

A graphic designer friend helped me design the CoThrive logo. It is based on the "three sisters"—corn, beans, and squash. Native Americans learned that these three thrive when planted together in one spot because each plant provides benefits to the others. The corn provides a vertical support for the climbing plants. The beans fix nitrogen from the air that the other plants need. The squash provides a natural mulch, cooling the roots of the other plants and helping to reduce weeds. Likewise, members do better when they plant themselves together rather than working as solopreneurs.

Social, By Nature

"Look deep into nature, and then you will understand everything better."
~ Albert Einstein

I have begun to use social permaculture design principles in all of my relationships, not just in business. As a Reiki Master, I have been very accustomed to healing with energy. Now, I map energy that flows between people in conversations and interactions. It has brought the social web to life for me in a new and exciting way, full of possibilities for co-creation.

Choosing the right business model and systems has healed my relationship to work. Even though I have never been happier in my work life, I often take "nature breaks" to continue learning from some of my best teachers, whether in a nearby forest or my own vegetable garden.

ABOUT THE AUTHOR: Kathy Sipple resides just outside of Chicago near the Indiana Dunes with her husband John and their black Labrador retriever, Bodhi. She is a frequent keynote speaker and trainer and host of 219 GreenConnect podcast. She holds a B.A. in Economics from the University of Michigan and is a member of Mensa. She won a Golden Innovator Award from Barbara Marx Hubbard and Conscious Evolutionaries Chicago-land for her empowering and groundbreaking work in social media. Sipple works online with clients everywhere to provide social media strategy, training, and coaching. For consulting info visit www.mysocialmediacoach.com or try her affordable group coaching program at www.cothrive.org.

Kathy Sipple
CoThrive
kathy@cothrive.org
cothrive.org
mysocialmediacoach.com

Is it Live or is it Memorex?
Leslie Miller Jewett

It was nearly midnight on the corner of Stillwell and Mermaid Avenues. As the waves crashed against the sand and the scent of cotton candy hung in the air—EMS frantically worked to save my brother's life.

They failed.

Rewind

November 2006.

It was my first night in a new apartment. Around 3:30 a.m. my phone started vibrating like crazy. I didn't recognize the number, so I ignored it and tried to go back to sleep. After the third or fourth time, I reached for the phone. There were missed calls from the same unfamiliar number, and they had finally left a message. It was the police calling to inform me that something had happened to my brother.

My heart sank as I clumsily dialed the call back number. He'd been mugged before and I envisioned him lying in the hospital bloodied and bruised—the victim of a gay bashing.

When the officer got on the line, he told me that my brother had passed away. He'd been walking home and collapsed. My only sibling had a heart attack at forty-one years old.

I heard myself saying something to the effect of: "Um…excuse me? Are you sure you have the right person? MY brother? I just saw him. He was fine!"

"I'm sorry," he replied robotically.

My brother and I had been next-door neighbors in Coney Island for the past three years. Memories of movie nights, laundry, food shopping, Nathan's Hot Dogs, fireworks, Denny's Ice Cream, and random rides on the Cyclone flooded my mind like a nightmarish movie montage.

I hung up the phone and let out a scream, as I fell to my knees. How was I going to tell my mom?

After losing my brother, New York seemed to lose its luster. The scene of so many happy memories had become just another painful reminder of his absence. When our lease was up a year later, my boyfriend and I moved to the two-family house just south of Boston where I had grown up. My parents still lived in the same apartment upstairs, so we took up residence on the first floor. I left behind my job in the music industry, its lucrative salary, and the identity I had created over the past fifteen years.

Being back triggered old childhood memories of being ostracized, socially inept, and wholly inadequate. Any sense of accomplishment or self-worth that I'd accumulated had completely vanished. I was a child again. Swell.

Fast Forward

I took a gig as a receptionist in a small veterinary hospital. Thanks to on-the-job training, I was still there five years later, working as a Technician.

It was August of 2012. Thursday was surgery day and by noon we had completed a neuter, a mass removal, and a couple of dental cleanings. I went into the break room to grab a snack and check my phone. When I saw several missed calls from my boyfriend, I got an awful feeling in the pit of my stomach. He never called me at work. I could hear the urgency in his voice as he said "Call me as soon as you get this."

Waiting for him to answer, my brain concocted every horrible scenario it could come up with—but not this one.

"Your dad's gone."

I vaguely remember driving home at top speed through a waterfall of tears.

Bursting through the front door, I wheezed, "Where is he? Where is he?"

By that time the police and funeral directors had been there for hours, and they had taken my daddy away. Feeling like I'd been abandoned, I cried hysterically while clutching my Mom. Why didn't he wait for me? How could they take him from me? I didn't even get to say good-bye!

My mother—always stoic—hugged me back. Her eyes bone dry she said, "What are we going to do now?"

Fast Forward

In June of 2013, after months of having trouble swallowing, I finally convinced my mom to go to the doctor. She refused to go sooner because "She didn't want to ruin our wedding." After my dad had passed, my other half and I decided we should tie the knot before we lost anyone else. Romantic, no?

She was diagnosed with esophageal cancer. The plan was to surgically insert a feeding tube, and once she recovered, begin three months of radiation and chemotherapy.

Mom finished her treatment at the end of October and by all indications, the tumor in her esophagus was gone. Her feeding tube was removed and we were able to have a fairly normal Thanksgiving and Christmas. But a few weeks later, she was having trouble again.

Since I was very young, I'd been obsessed with what happens to us physically, mentally, and spiritually when we die. I read everything I could get my hands on that was even remotely related. For the longest time, I thought I was just a morbid little creep. But as it turned out, I was preparing myself.

An exploratory endoscopy was scheduled and during the procedure, they discovered a fistula between her esophagus and windpipe. She had been aspirating everything she was eating and drinking, including her saliva, which resulted in pneumonia. The doctor decided to place a stent in her throat to try to impede the aspiration.

She was admitted for observation and awoke in a great deal of pain. This was incredibly disturbing to me because I had never heard my mother complain. I knew it had to be bad.

She refused to take anything orally, so another feeding tube was placed. I was told she would have to rely on it for the rest of her life. A couple of days later, as the doctors were discussing her discharge, they discovered that one of her lungs had filled with fluid. When a drain was inserted to relieve the pressure, the lung collapsed. It was her third time under anesthesia in two weeks.

At that point, I said—enough! Step away from the nice lady.

She had been through so much already and everything they tried just seemed to make things worse. I know she didn't want this, so I made the decision to call in hospice.

Three weeks to the day after she went in for a routine procedure, my mother quietly passed away, my husband and I at her side. It was the most horribly wonderful experience of my life.

Fast Forward

My family was gone. The people I loved transformed into decorative wooden boxes on display in my living room. And what was to come of me? I had no idea.

For years I'd shaped myself into what I thought I was supposed to be, depending on who I was with. I realized that I'd spent so much time pretending to be someone else that I had no clue who I actually was. All I knew for sure was that I was no longer a sister or a daughter and didn't know how to process that.

The months after mom passed were a blur, spent largely on autopilot. I returned to work, but micromanagement and my state-of-mind proved to be a noxious combination. I walked out twelve days before Christmas.

I knew I had to get another job, but had no idea where to begin. I needed something less stressful and more supportive than my last place of employment. So, I turned to the kind folks at the metaphysical store where I'd learned about reiki, meditation, chakras, intuition, and mediumship. It seemed like the perfect place, at least until I could figure out what I wanted to be when I grew up.

Shortly after I began working there, I was asked for a favor. The yoga teacher training class needed an even number of people for a workshop and would I mind sitting in? I had never done yoga in my life and I'm possibly the least flexible person, with the worst balance, on the planet. But for reasons unbeknownst to me at the time, I said yes.

When I arrived, there were about fifteen women sitting on the wooden floor of a loft-style room. I looked around and realized immediately that I was way out of my comfort zone. The anxiety was making me nauseous, and it was about to get a whole lot worse.

As we began, we learned that the day was all about self-inquiry. We were to choose a question to ponder: Who or what am I? Then spend approximately fifteen minutes with each person in the room alternately answering our chosen question, while maintaining eye contact at all times. You were only to speak when it was your turn and otherwise remain silent for the duration of the day.

What had I gotten myself into?

It started with the obvious pleasantries: I'm a wife. I'm a friend. I'm a pug mom. Yada, yada, yada.

Then we moved on to self-deprecation:

I am ugly. I am stupid. I am not worthy of being loved.

During our lunch break, I rehashed everything I'd said and continued to ponder the question internally. Naturally, this was the perfect time to plunge head first into the depths of despair:

I am lost. I am afraid. I am alone. I am…utterly alone.

At this point, an intense, cyclic breathing exercise was introduced into the mix. Lying on the floor, desperately trying not to panic—inhale, exhale, inhale, exhale, inhale, exhale—I just know I'm going hyperventilate and die.

But then, something started to happen. My head felt like it was full of red-hot pins and needles. The warmth traveled down my body in a wave of white light that felt like being hugged by pure love. Finally, I heard six words that changed my life:

Other people do not define you.

We paired up one last time. Only now, everything had changed. I looked deeply into my partner's eyes and said:

"I am aware. I am transformed. I am free!"

I burst into tears and realized that although technically I was a daughter, sister, wife, and friend, they were just labels I'd imposed upon myself based on my relationships. I'd always despised when others labeled me, yet I'd thought nothing of doing so to myself.

You are who you are, whether anyone else is around or not. And even if someone is around, said someone doesn't make you any less you!

But fear is a tricky little bugger. Almost every block I've discovered in myself is in one way or another based in fear. Some people deny their fear and put on their strong-like-bull façade to go out into the world. But when they go home, they eat a pint of ice cream and lie on the couch in the fetal position, wondering where the hell time had gone—just like the rest of us.

I believe that fear, as much as it sucks, is a very useful emotion. It gives us pause to contemplate what we're about to say or do and the potential consequences of those words or actions. The problem begins when you let fear prevent you from doing something because you think someone might make fun of you or because you think you won't be good at it or heaven forbid, you might embarrass yourself. True strength comes when you feel that fear and you persist anyway! Who you are and who you can become is limited only by your own imagination.

Sure, we all seek validation from others, but it's important to remember that their perception is subjective and likely has more to do with their previous experiences than actually with you. And I'll let you in on a little secret…other people don't pay attention to us as much as we think they do! They have their own stuff they're freaking out about.

So, now whenever anyone tries to put me in a box (myself included), I turn the crank, pop right out, and dance to the music with a big ole smile on my face!

ABOUT THE AUTHOR: Recovering alcoholic and self-proclaimed "walking contradiction", Leslie Miller Jewett, has battled depression and anxiety for as long as she can remember. After discovering she is empathic, she studied different healing modalities and is now a Certified Zentangle Teacher® and Reiki Master. With a focus on art, meditation, and energy work, Leslie hopes that sharing her knowledge and experiences will inspire others to embrace their unique qualities and help them to become comfortable in their own skin. She is the owner of ZENSQRL and lives on Boston's South Shore with her husband and two pugs.

Leslie Miller Jewett
leslie@lesliemillerjewett.com
lesliemillerjewett.com
facebook.com/zensqrl/
etsy.com/shop/ZENSQRL

Are You My Guru?
Amy Jayalakshmi Hellman

Teaching has always come naturally to me. It wasn't something I had to train for or stress out about, it was just an ability I was gifted with. Perhaps because it was so easy, for many years I resisted honing my skills, instead basing my decisions on what people told me I *should* be and how I *ought* to think. I listened to others blindly, never questioning their perspectives. This is the story of what happened when I met my guru and realized how unprepared I was for all she had to show me. This is the story of my *real* training to become a teacher.

After graduate school in Europe, I returned to New York City and worked as a teacher and tutor. My parents, in an effort to reconnect me with my younger sister, enrolled us in a bodywork training at the Sivananda Ashram in the Bahamas. Vianna Stibal, founder of The ThetaHealing® Technique, was there teaching. I attended her talks each night and found her both funny and brilliant. As she spoke about quantum physics and the mind, and how magical and powerful our thoughts were, she validated something that had been dormant inside me; a sense of ease wrapped around me like a warm blanket, and I knew I exactly where I was supposed to be.

When the following year I returned to the ashram for a yoga teacher training, I was delighted to find that Vianna was there as well. I also received quite a shock during an Ayurvedic consultation. This is in many ways similar to a doctor's physical; however, it also includes a diagnosis of one's dominant constitutional attributes, an analysis if it can go out of balance, and what to do about it. I was told my diagnosis of Bipolar disorder was incorrect.

"You are not bipolar, Amy," she said, "You have relatives in your family who have bipolar disorder, surely, but you, *you* are empathic. You have just never learned how to use it properly. You need to learn how to *be you* with your gifts." In that instant, Ayurveda, an Indian science of healing dating back more than two thousand years, stripped away the false self-image I'd been holding for years. In its place was the woman I actually was, and she was powerful. The doctor had confirmed an ever-present yet indescribable feeling that had been with me my entire life: that there was more of me than I had access to. This closeted self had been shouting through my skin, and now she was here. I returned to New York City, a new person, determined to take a ThetaHealing class that April.

Acclimatizing to my daily life proved difficult. My fiancé and I struggled to reorient our relationship with the person I was becoming. To cope, I joined a yoga center in Manhattan, teaching classes and apprenticing with the resident swami. This was helpful, but "real" life kept creeping in. One afternoon, my mother called to tell me her marriage to my father was finished. This was not news; she had been considering the idea since I was ten, even casually asking, "Should I divorce your father?"

"This time, Amy, it is real," she whispered into the phone.

"This time," my father told me, "I'm not sure we are going to make it."

Both called me regularly that winter. After a lifetime of self-medicating for his Bipolar and colitis symptoms, my father went to rehab. My mother's latent anger at having to wait thirty years for him to do so consumed her. As always, I listened to every step of her journey, until one day, I was abruptly and irrevocably done.

"Mom, stop!" I shouted, not caring that I was standing in the street in SoHo, "I can't listen to this anymore. Please don't call me again until you can keep it to yourself."

I then hung up on her. Hanging up on my mother would soon become the new norm.

Around this time, things at the yoga center also changed. The swami became argumentative, bullying volunteers, and asking questions that were inappropriate. Thankfully, he left to return to civilian life. Then, just when it seemed life was getting back to normal, I got sick.

There was nothing remarkable about this cold, no indicators it would wreak havoc on my life, work, or relationships. It was just a "bug" going around school. It was nothing.

Until it became something.

Until the cold outstayed its welcome, and three weeks later, moved from my sinuses to my ears.

Until that cold immersed me in the soft, dense quiet of deafness to the outside world.

Until that cold introduced to me my own thoughts, which were deafening.

There was nothing I could do; I had no way of triaging the disaster flooding my mind, no way to ignore or fight it.

The loneliness was overwhelming. While the external auditory world didn't disappear entirely, it seemed a world away. It was as if I was underwater and had forgotten how to resurface. I had finally discovered my Self, and I was drowning in her.

The first doctor diagnosed an ear infection; when treatment failed, she diagnosed allergies. When that failed, an ENT administered a hearing test, which, oddly enough, showed neither significant hearing loss nor physical damage to my ears. *What was going on?* He blew pressurized air into my nose, and I emerged for ten seconds before being swallowed again by the deafening lake of my Self.

I was given a litany of suggestions from various healthcare providers, and I sampled them all: steroids prescribed by the ENT; cranial-sacral therapy for the Temporomandibular Joint Dysfunction (TMJ) caused by the phantom pressure in my ears; and acupuncture treatments that helped my hearing but wore off after five hours. I changed my diet, cleaned my liver, kidneys, and colon; I did parasite cleanses. I saw a psychic; I got serious about healing my Self. I wrote poetry again. Through it all, my hearing did not improve; I simply got better at pretending I could hear. Teaching was embarrassing and wounded my pride; I took a leave of absence from teaching yoga and faked hearing through the rest of the schoolyear. Even watching TV was stressful—a crippling reminder that I could not participate in the world despite being told

I was "fine" by everyone in authority.

I was more isolated than ever; the only relationship I really had access to was the one with myself, and I did not speak my own language. But I was learning.

It was early summer when I was walking through Barnes & Noble and "ThetaHealing" jumped off the shelf. It reminded me of the April class I had been so excited about taking when I returned from the ashram but never made it to. *Well,* I thought, *now's as good a time as ever to see what I missed.*

Each day I'd take the book and lay on the hammock given to me by middle school students on a trip to Costa Rica a few years back. Every few pages, I'd stop and close my eyes. Since my hearing loss, I had been forced to be alone with myself; now, for the first time I began in earnest to communicate with her.

Slowly but deliberately, I went through all the steps, just as if I was in the class. I learned the basic practice of inducing a theta brain wave while staying awake and connecting to the subatomic energy of creation, the energy we call unconditional love.

At the time, I had no religious, spiritual, or emotional vocabulary for what I was doing every day in my backyard. I did not grow up with a belief that God, or creator—or anyone else for that matter—would help me learn. I had to do it myself. I kept reading and practicing. If I stopped, I was bombarded by my thoughts, so I didn't stop. As I practiced, the exercises helped me understand how to direct my thoughts, how to organize them, and even, how to change them.

I became my own best student. I finished the book and reread it twice more going further. Things started happening. My relationships changed; my fiancé and I grew closer. I planned two trips to visit my father and grandparents in Arizona. I felt happier. I also felt gratitude to the practice for offering me a "place to go," where I could imagine who I wanted to become each day, and I was starting to see her appear in my physical reality.

Yet, my ears were no clearer. Was I losing my mind? Frustrated, I muttered, "What do I need to do to heal my ears?!" The answer came gently, like the waves of Long Island Sound that lapped against the shore by my childhood window. I realized that it had been playing for some time, I'd just been too busy panicking to hear it.

"Write a letter to your mother."

I remember sitting in my grandparent's house in Arizona, trying to force this letter. When words failed, my throat grew heavy with rage. *"What an idiot I am, to believe that it could be that easy."*

Strange, then, that my mother's sister should arrive that day for an impromptu visit from L.A. Just five feet tall and ninety pounds, she was also a barracuda of an attorney. It seemed we'd barely said hello when she proceeded to march me to the front porch and yell into my face, "You can't let your silly parents' drama keep you from your purpose, Amy. You are meant for so much. Start finding your mentors. Write them letters!"

A few weeks later, I sat in the back of my sister's minivan with her and her family, my body sluggish from the Missouri humidity. It was Guru Purnima, a holiday to honor your teachers; my nephews were busy chattering away with one another, so I asked again, *"How do I heal my ears?"*

The answer was the same. Then came my thoughts, angry plates of ice colliding into one another over the sea of my deafness, screeching through the serenity I'd been trying to cultivate all summer.

"But I can't write my mother! And why aren't I well yet? I'm so disappointed in myself. How will I work in the fall? I'm going to have to do something else, but what? I have no skills. I'm a failure. I'm spending so much time meditating people are going to lock me up. How come no one is helping me? I'm doing all the right things, and no one seems to be able to help me get better! Am I crazy? Where are all the teachers I am supposed to be learning from? Who the hell are my teachers? Who the hell is this mother you keep telling me to write? What is her name?!"

A gentle laughter consumed me; I looked around, thinking someone else was laughing. Very clearly, as if I *finally* I was asking the right questions, I heard the name, *"Vianna."* Afraid and pretty certain I was losing my mind, it took me one week to write the letter.

I wrote with sparkly gel ink on sketchbook paper, not for

Vianna, but for myself. I wrote it as I wanted to read it. I shared with my teacher every part of this journey, and how afraid I was to get well, of who I was nervous—but ready—to become. When I was done, the letter folded into a self-contained envelope and walked from my house the four blocks to the post box next to the Burger King by the Brooklyn-Queens Expressway. When I opened the mail slot, my letter slid in, and before I had time to think, the lid slammed shut; there was a pop, and out of instinct, I dropped down to the ground to protect myself.

Suddenly, I could hear the cars honking as they drove under the bridge on the BQE. I could hear the truck's transmission drop as he pulled up to order a sandwich from the drive-thru. I could hear what had always been there these past four months that I was under water. I stood up then, looked around at the people walking by me, smiled, and walked home.

Over the next three days, my hearing continued to improve and never left.

I was born with many gifts, not just teaching. Listening to others transformed into the ability to listen to myself. It was time I began using it. I was ready.

ABOUT THE AUTHOR: Amy J.'s journey as a teacher began over twenty years ago, when she realized that teaching was learning transformed. Since then she has had the pleasure of instructing students of all ages and backgrounds and on topics ranging from academic to self-healing and more. Amy holds a master's degree from the University of Oxford and a Masters and Certificate of Science from the ThetaHealing Institute of Knowledge; she uses her extensive background in academic instruction and the healing arts to guide families and teachers looking for pathways to success for their children and students.

Amy Jayalakshmi
Manna Healing with Amy J.
manna-healing.com
amy@manna-healing.com
706-804-2695

Finding the Gift in Loss
Sherry Rueger Banaka

In 1978, just three months after his second birthday, my only child drowned. Paramedics were able to resuscitate his breathing and heartbeat, but Robin remained unconscious. He was in critical care for two weeks, until on June 15, 1978, his organs began to fail. My husband, Randy, and I were advised to say our last words and to make the decision to stop all life support. Though painfully difficult, it was clear to me that Robin was no longer present. Whereas a few hours before, his little body had color and held a sense of life, it was now a pale, lifeless shell.

That night, as we returned home and entered our bedroom, my eyes focused on crayon figures Robin had drawn on the wall. I remembered being irritated with him at the time, but now I knelt down, saying softly, "Oh, Robin." I reached out and touched his drawing and instantly felt his arms around my waist.

Turning to look, I saw Robin hovering above me, no longer flesh and blood, but there just the same. With him was a purple-robed figure I instinctively knew was a guide. I heard Robin's words in my mind, "Everything's okay. I have to go now." And with that, he and the guide were gone.

I was twenty-six years old. I believed that Robin's drowning was my fault and Randy blamed me too. Though family and friends tried to comfort me, I felt isolated and alone, with no one to confide in and no one to help me understand my feelings. Mostly I was numb, though I clearly remember feeling very angry. I was furious at Randy's lack of support and blame. We divorced two years later.

I spent the next several years going from relationship to relationship, anything to keep from feeling my grief, anguish, guilt, and shame. Then in 1992 Chuck Banaka came into my life. We had actually been introduced many years earlier, but now I had the opportunity to get to know him and become friends. On March 21, 1997, Chuck and I were married.

Chuck was a very gentle, intelligent, sensitive man who was always there for me. We were committed to one another, and I felt safe and loved. Then in October 2009, the unthinkable happened. Chuck was diagnosed with stage IV, inoperable lung cancer.

We joined a cancer support group that was instrumental in helping us maintain a positive outlook. Chuck underwent radiation and chemotherapy, complementing those with acupuncture and Naturopathic care. But despite our efforts, by July 2012, the cancer had "blossomed," spreading throughout his body like dust in the wind.

Chuck was admitted to Hopewell House Hospice Hospital, where he received loving, palliative care, and I was allowed to remain by his side. On July 29, 2012, the nurses alerted me that Chuck's body had begun to transition and encouraged me to climb into bed with him. I glanced at the clock; it was 11:50 p.m. As I lay there, listening to the steady rhythm of Chuck's heartbeat, I must have dozed. Suddenly, I was startled by the hiss of oxygen and looked at the clock. It was 11:55 p.m. I listened again, still hearing nothing but that hiss. Chuck had stopped breathing. I called for the nurse, and at 12:05 a.m., my beloved husband was pronounced dead.

During those six days at Hopewell House, I had felt such a sense of grace and peace. But coming home alone afterward, I was raw with pain and shock. Knowing I needed help, I found a bereavement support group, where I learned that to heal, we must face our grief and learn to move through it, not over, under, or around it. I also found that losing Chuck had brought my grief over Robin's death to the surface, and I would have to face those emotions as well.

For the next year and a half, the pain remained acute. Thankfully the bereavement support group also taught me that this is normal. Bursts of grief come in waves. It often feels like we are going backward when we are really on a spiral of healing. If we are actively mourning, that is.

Perhaps the most important thing I learned is there is a difference between grieving and mourning. Grief is the internal experience of the loss of our loved ones. Mourning is the outward expression of it, through crying, talking, writing, drawing, or whatever expressive outlet we might find. It is through mourning that we heal, and it cannot be rushed or trivialized.

As author, educator, and grief counselor Alan D. Wolfelt, PhD explained:

"Many people in grief have internalized society's message that mourning should be done quietly, quickly, and efficiently. Such messages encourage the repression of the griever's thoughts and feelings. The problem is that attempting to mask or move away from grief results in internal anxiety and confusion. With little, if any, social recognition of the normal pain of grief, people begin to think their thoughts and feelings are abnormal. "I think I'm going crazy," they often tell me. They're not crazy, just grieving. And in order to heal they must move toward their grief through continued mourning, not away from it through repression and denial."[1]

Eighteen months after Chuck's death, I discovered a wonderful new tool to help me mourn: Emotional Freedom Techniques (EFT). I learned how to literally "tap" into the deep, dark places inside me where my guilt, regret and shame lived in the shadows, bring them into the light of my own awareness, acknowledge them, and release them. With EFT, I was able to face and heal these painful emotions more quickly. And now, when I feel the sorrow of loss, I'm able to simply tap and move through it into love and gratitude.

So, how does EFT do this? Tapping gently connects us with our painful inner memories and emotions, even the ones we may not be fully aware of, and brings them safely into our conscious awareness. Holding them in our awareness while tapping on key acupressure points sends soothing signals to our brains. The stress response is halted and disengaged as our bodies release healthful hormones that relax us and allow us to feel calm and at peace.

This does not heal the loss itself; however, it does help us heal the painful emotions surrounding the loss. As we alleviate that pain, our focus shifts to the good memories and to gratitude for the love we shared.

With EFT, my healing and personal growth have expanded exponentially. I can only wonder what impact it might have had on my ability to be more fully present with Chuck, to support him even more through his illness and dying process, and to help us both with all the overwhelming thoughts and emotions we were experiencing. How much more quickly might I have been able to release the guilt, regret, anger, remorse, and fear I carried after he died?

While I've used other energy techniques—guided imagery and visualization, meditation and mindfulness, and have found they work wonderfully together—EFT has had the most visible and dramatic impact. With it, I have discovered and released many painful emotions I was still carrying from old, often mistaken, beliefs. These were not just about the shock, emptiness, despair, and other feelings associated with the deaths of my loved ones. Tapping has also helped me heal many childhood wounds, while strengthening my self-esteem, my trust in my instincts and intuition, and my sense of connection with the universal energy we all share.

In the years since Chuck's death, I've had many experiences of his eternal energy. The morning after he died, just as I awoke and opened my eyes, I saw Chuck lying in bed facing me, smiling and holding my hands in his. Just a brief glimpse, and then he was gone. I've also seen his light body standing at the foot of our bed, and I've had sudden insights about what to do after asking for his help.

On our first wedding anniversary after Chuck's death, I decided to take some of his ashes to Leach Botanical Garden, where we were married. On the way, the traffic was unusually heavy and the drive unusually long. I was listening to All Classical FM on the radio and noticed the music was exceptionally beautiful. Once I arrived, I spent time walking the grounds and leaving ashes in various spots that were meaningful to Chuck and me. Then, on the drive home, the traffic was again very heavy. All Classical FM was still playing exquisite music, the likes of which I had never heard before.

When I arrived home, I went immediately to Chuck's portrait and said, "Happy Anniversary, Honey." And then it struck me. The night before, I had been with a group of friends, one of whom is a medium. She had said to me, "Chuck asked me to tell you he wants to play some beautiful music for you." I looked up at his portrait and whispered, "Thank you for your beautiful anniversary gift to me." Chuck smiled. Right there in the portrait, he smiled.

My most recent gift from Chuck came on New Year's Day 2017, which would have been his sixty-sixth birthday. I was spending the day with my sisters, Donna and Glenda. Glenda had invited us to her house for a small ceremony to welcome in the healing energy of the Divine Mother and release the old energies of 2016.

Over the past four years I had been releasing Chuck's ashes in places that held significance for us. This year, as his birthday approached, I felt this would be the year to release the rest of them, and in doing so, complete this part of my healing process.

So, when the ceremony reached the point of releasing the old, I poured Chuck's ashes into the flowerbeds all along the back wall of Glenda's garden. A powerful and unexpected surge of energy flowed through me, and I wept profusely with sorrow and gratitude. When I had finished releasing the ashes, I rose up—spontaneously and unplanned—and caressed each and every plant that had received some of Chuck's ashes, blessing each one to receive this nourishment from his body and use it to create abundant new life. Tears and intensely powerful energy were pouring through me the entire time, and when the blessings were done, I felt an abiding, cleansing release and peace. Chuck had been there with me, joining his energy with mine. A profoundly beautiful New Year's Day, and an unanticipated gift for which I am enormously grateful.

During the four-and-a-half years since his death, I have received many gifts from Chuck, always letting me know his energy is alive and well, just in a different way. His gift to me this New Year's Day was the latest, and I felt he was encouraging me to follow my instincts and finally release what I hadn't been ready yet to relinquish, including the rest of his ashes and belongings, and even the house we bought and lived in together.

Am I completely healed? My experience is that I have traveled far on the upward spiral of healing, from the depths of raw and buried pain to a heart filled with love and gratitude. I thank Robin for being my sweet child those few short years; I thank Chuck for everything he gave me in all our time together—his love, patience, and wisdom, his acts of gentle, loving kindness; and I thank them both for their final sacrifice, with all the gifts that have come from it.

I had never really grasped the story of Jesus dying on the cross, was not even sure I believed it really happened. Besides the more obvious message of life after death, I now understand that death is a *gift*. It is a sacrifice we have the opportunity to learn from in order to expand ourselves, to awaken, to begin to *truly live*.

At some point, whether it's tomorrow or thirty years from now, it will be my turn to die. I do not want to waste this gift given me by the deaths of my loved ones. I want to live, I want to love, I want to give. I want to be authentic and fully present, embracing and embodying my highest potential and purpose. I cannot allow myself to do or to be anything less.

Sources
[1] Alan D. Wolfett, Ph.D., *Helping Dispel 5 Common Myths About Grief* (griefwords.com)
griefwords.com/index.cgi?action=page&page=articles%2Fhelping7.html&site _id=5

ABOUT THE AUTHOR: The tremendous help Sherry received from EFT to process her grief over the deaths of her child and husband inspired her to become an EFT/Energy Practitioner. She was personally trained and mentored by Dawson Church, PhD, and is certified through his organization, EFT Universe, to practice Clinical EFT, the method validated by dozens of clinical trials. It is Sherry's passion and privilege to help others learn and benefit from this easy to use self-help tool that is so effective in alleviating the stressful responses associated with loss and other life events. She offers EFT/Energy sessions in person and online.

Sherry Rueger Banaka
sherryruegerbanaka.com
sherryruegerbanaka@gmail.com
503-347-4974

Seimei and the Skeptic
Kathy Leone

The first time Delores called me, I almost didn't answer. I was driving at the time and a quick glance at my cell told me it wasn't a friend or family member. But I'd learned long ago to listen to my intuition, and right now it was telling me to pull over and take the call.

"Hi," a woman said hesitantly, "My name is Dolores and I was given your name by Carol, a psychic, who told me you could help me."

Delores told me she'd had been suffering with severe sciatica for over nine months. During that time it had gotten progressively worse, and was now to the point where there was almost no position—walking, sitting, standing, laying down—when she didn't feel pain in the right buttocks and leg.

Dolores was in her mid-seventies and had never worked with a holistic practitioner. "Kathy, I have to be honest with you. I don't really believe in what you do or that you can help me, but I am desperate."

I understood exactly where she was coming from. Twenty-five years earlier, I had felt the same way when I was suffering from a debilitating health issue and getting no relief from the medical community. There was, however, one major difference between Dolores and myself: I *was* a Holistic Practitioner. I'd studied and practiced massage therapy, Reiki, and Classical Homeopathy. And I was going to holistic therapists at the time, which had helped me with other health issues, but no course of treatment worked well enough to get me feeling better and functioning again, and I fell into a deep depression. Looking back, I realize it was a turning point, but at the time it just felt like more suffering in a life that had been filled with it.

I was not a healthy child. At just two months old I was being treated for urinary tract infections. I also had numerous sinus infections, ear infections, strep throat, and then more serious issues. I contracted Mono, pneumonia, and then Scarlet Fever. I didn't have much energy, had difficulty digesting, struggled with depression, and began self-medicating as a teenager. I was given antibiotics every day for six weeks to help with yet another UTI but all I got was Chronic Candida. My health went downhill quickly.

The combination of never feeling well and wanting to help others led me towards natural solutions. I began taking vitamins and eating healthier. I quit drinking and led a cleaner life. Yet, by age twenty-eight I had hit a wall. I had no energy, difficulty breathing and swallowing, and my arms hung limp at my side. I found several chiropractors who helped me get out of bed and work part time, but I was still functioning minimally. Most frustrating of all was that the doctors could not come up with a formal diagnosis. One neurologist suggested I get a cleaning lady and use paper plates so I didn't have to do the dishes! Now you can see why I was so depressed. I had given up on myself.

Then a good friend, Gerry, called to tell me about a new therapy she was bringing her son to called The Actions of Seimei. Gerry asked if I wanted to try it, and though it sounded intriguing I said no. I was afraid of another disappointment. But Gerry persisted, asking me on several other occasions to check it out, until one day I said yes. I told her—and myself—that I was only going because she wanted my opinion on how it was helping her son with his medical condition. I managed to get myself to a local bookstore where they were giving free demonstrations of the technique.

I walked into the room to find several Seimei practitioners, along with about twelve other people there to learn about the treatment. We were asked to pick one point of pain we were having at the moment. Immediately, my mind went into overdrive. How could I pick just one pain? My body literally hurt from head to toe. My neck and shoulders were stiff, my arms were heavy and I was exhausted. If the situation wasn't so dire I might have found it comical. I had no expectation whatsoever of feeling better, right up until the practitioner put her hands level with my neck about six inches away from body. Within thirty seconds my neck and shoulders relaxed and almost all of my pain was gone! Astounded, I jumped out of the chair and drove myself home. I walked in the door and cleaned my whole house, all the while contemplating what had happened in that bookstore. I didn't think it would last forever; in fact, the practitioner had told me it would last for three days and that I would probably need Seimei sessions. For the time being all I cared about was that I felt normal and HOPEFUL. I waited about two weeks, when my symptoms began appearing again, then called to schedule my first session.

With each Seimei session I noticed my health and mood improving, and I just knew I had to learn how to do this to help myself and others. When the first official class was held in the United States, I was there. That was in March of 1997. I never went back to giving massages, even though I would have been physically able to. The speed and depth with which I could use Seimei to help others amazed me. It also satisfied a spiritual longing as it helped me to access my Divine self in a way I wasn't previously able to.

Part of the process is making people comfortable by explaining what I do and how sick I was. While Dolores was perhaps the first person with the courage to tell me she didn't believe in what I did, I have deep compassion for all my clients and an understanding of what they are going through. I assure them that if I recovered, so can they.

Delores had many questions on the phone that day, and I took them one by one, trying to put her at ease. To make it even more confusing for her, the session was going to be remote since I lived in New Jersey and she lived roughly five hours away in New York State. There was no guarantee I could help her and I knew it would be a tremendous leap of faith for her to trust me. We spoke for a little while longer, then Dolores said she was going to get her second epidural and see if that helped before she decided whether to work with me.

One week later Dolores called me back. The epidural had done nothing to ease her discomfort. She was still very skeptical but told me she had nothing to lose and would try one session. I really wanted to help her—I could hear how much she was suffering—but I was also apprehensive because I didn't know how many sessions it would take. Dolores had a herniated disc in her lumbar spine, and so far nothing had helped her. If I couldn't, she was going to need surgery. We set up her session for the following Monday morning, with the understanding that she would call to check in with me beforehand.

When she called that Monday, I asked, "On a scale of one to ten, how bad is your pain when you walk? Stand? Sit? Lay down? Bend over? And how far can you walk until it stops you?" Delores reported that she could take one step and it was unbearable. Finally, I asked her to state her intention for the session: "Take away my pain so I can walk again." When I had all of the info I needed to begin, we hung up. Dolores was going to try to rest in her recliner while I headed to my meditation room. I was going to try to help her walk.

I began meditating and connecting to Source energy and the energy of the healing angels and masters. Then I asked for Dolores to be present in her energetic form. I scanned her body with my hands as if she was sitting in a chair in front of me. I felt many different sensations as I went all around her body looking for the blockages. I could feel the herniated disc and the inflammation in the nerves on the right side of her body. I could also feel some emotional issue encapsulating the disc.

The first thing I did was release the emotions so I could get a clearer picture of the disc. After it let go, I kept my hands in place to help shift the energy of the actual disc. My job was to locate where the blockages were stored and surrender so Source could activate her ability to heal herself. After a half hour, I noticed less pain in my hands so I called to check in. Dolores told me that she felt more relaxed in other places but the pain had intensified! I assured her this is part of the process and would continue with the session and check back in shortly.

Again, I felt a lessening of sensations in my hands so I called Dolores back. I asked her to walk since that was when she felt the most pain. "I will walk as far as I can until the pain stops me," she said. Instead of feeling it with her first step like before the session, she was able to walk all the way across the room with only a few twinges of pain. She acknowledged improvement but admitted she had a difficult time believing it had anything to do with our session. I understood why she would think this and it didn't bother me. Before we hung up, I told her that changes would occur for another three days. During this cycle, she would likely experience bouts of more pain followed by none.

"Please take care of yourself and call me to let me know how you are doing." I knew I could help her more but left it up to her to decide if or when.

Several weeks later I heard back from Dolores. She sounded different, more relaxed. The first three days after the session had indeed been rough, but she was happy to report that since then the pain had decreased by about fifty percent. Dolores was encouraged that with more sessions, she would experience more relief. We scheduled another appointment and the session was similar to the first one. She felt her body changing during the session and was looking forward to feeling good after the three days. In the meantime, she'd scheduled the surgery for three weeks out. She didn't want to do it but was still going to go through the pre-op testing just in case. I was thrilled she had gotten so much relief and hoped for her sake that she didn't need the surgery.

One week later, we worked together again for the third time. Her life had been more normal than it had been in the previous nine months. She was able to watch her grandchildren play ball again, go shopping, and sleep better—all promising signs. I repeated the process for her session and no longer felt so much inflammation in her disc and nerves. As with the other sessions, she felt things shift during the session. She still had surgery scheduled and had not made up her mind whether to cancel it.

After that, weeks went by with no word from Dolores, and I assumed she had the surgery. Then I got a call. When she went for the pre-op MRI, it showed she long longer had a herniated disc! She was also completely free of the sciatica pain and had cancelled the operation.

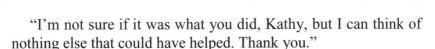

"I'm not sure if it was what you did, Kathy, but I can think of nothing else that could have helped. Thank you."

Since then Dolores has referred people to me. Sometimes the biggest skeptics turn out to be the biggest believers. I know, because I am living proof.

ABOUT THE AUTHOR: Kathy Leone is an Intuitive Catalyst for healing and change. Kathy has always been sensitive to the needs of others, which led her to study and practice many forms of healing, including Massage Therapy, Reiki, Classical Homeopathy, and Access Bars. While on her path she fell seriously ill and experienced her most profound healing from the Seimei technique. In 1997 Kathy trained in the Seimei method, first in the USA, then Japan. She is a former Seimei Instructor and managed The Seimei Foundation for many years. Kathy combines all of her expertise to get at the root cause of illness, release blockages, and create profound shifts wherever her clients need it most.

Kathy Leone
Holistic Practitioner
KathyLeone.com
kathyseimei@optonline.net

The Cherry Blossom Channel
Robin VanHorn Schwoyer

"WTH! Can anything else go wrong?!" I stomped outside. The breath of fresh air might have felt good, if I was actually breathing deeply and not just huffing in an anxious state. My head ached. My heart was pounding in my ears. I felt tears but pushed them aside and began walking.

Several blocks later, I heard a noise... an unusual yet distantly familiar sound. It captured my imagination, and I tried to imitate it but couldn't. I knew it was some sort of animal. Not a bird. What was this sound—part-trill, part-warble? Then it hit me! A tree frog! Living in the North, I had not heard a tree frog in a long time.

I flashed to a childhood road trip through Georgia and Florida with my family. I just loved the lush look, the fragrances, and the sounds. I especially, loved the tree frogs. They felt magical to me.

So, here I am, a few blocks from my house, trying to imitate a tree frog and wondering what it looked like. I felt my anxiety slip away as I focused on this unseen creature. As I listened more, I realized I heard a call and response. There were more tree frogs! They were answering each other.

Oddly, at that moment I found myself wishing I *were* a tree frog. Their lives had to be easier. Then again, they had their challenges—living outdoors, in the elements, having to find food, and avoid becoming food for other creatures. I sat on the curb under a tree, just listening. I relaxed into this space, feeling the rhythm of the frogs' calls. My mind wandered away from my earlier concerns. I tuned into the colors around me. The trees were becoming greener, and there were all of these pinkish white blossoms. A Cherry Tree was flowering above me. I felt my spirits lift.

Then a voice spoke. I looked around, but saw no one. This was fine with me—I wasn't in the mood for human interaction, I just wanted to focus on the frogs and blossoms.

Suddenly, an older man appeared from behind a large bush. "So, you decided to take refuge here by the Cherry Tree?"

"Well, I heard the tree frogs and was enjoying their songs," I replied, "Yes, I guess I took refuge here on the curb under the tree."

"I find a lot of people under this tree," the old man informed me, and I looked around to see where exactly I was. I had been walking, my head down, in a locomotive-driven state of agitation.

"These trees used to be part of the farm that was here," the man shared, "The farmer sold when he got too old, and lots of the groves were removed to make way for houses."

I took a moment to study him. He was an older man, but something felt timeless about him. His eyes had a gleam, and a vocal tone that was soothing. I smiled and asked if it was okay for me to sit here. He moved closer and stood in front of me. He looked deeply into my eyes as I looked up at him, and I felt this amazing sense of embrace. Not a physical hug, but a presence of love and peace. "What troubles you?" he asked.

I felt the tears well up. I explained I was caring for my father who was ill and close to death, my kids had been sick for a few days—even the dogs were suffering from some stomach bug. Bills were piling up and things needed repair. A friend had died, and other friends seemed to disappear as I needed to spend more time tending to my father.

The man smiled compassionately. "So, you heard the frogs?"

"Yes," I replied as I smiled, dropping my eyes to the few petals on the ground beside me.

He gave me a comical smirk. "Do you know what frog stands for?"

I looked up at him.

"F-R-O-G," he said, spelling out the word, then explained, "Fully Rely On God."

Ah yes, I had a memory of earlier years in Sunday School, and then when I was teaching at the Church. FROG!

"You needed to take a break. I'm glad you found my tree. They call me Anthony. Take as much time as you need, but remember to take care of yourself all the time. You can't wait until your head is exploding and heart aching so much. You know what to do; I can see your Spirit. You help others all the time. You like to teach too. What would you tell yourself right now?" Anthony asked, and I felt the strange warm glow embracing me again.

I looked up, and the Cherry Tree Blossoms were moving in a breeze above me. The small green leaves flickered as well. It felt like a Morse code of information was flowing as the branches moved and the petals sparkled with delicate lights.

My heart space expanded as I deeply sighed. My mind softly flooded with golden light, tones, and images—there were messages for myself and for others. Clarity and inspiration illumined what had been a dense and dark sensation only moments before.

Yes, what would I tell myself? Lately, my Self-talk sounded critical and down. I was a natural optimist, but these past months of constant care-giving and problem-solving had somehow shifted this perspective.

I looked again at this gentleman, this messenger named Anthony, and I smiled from a more joyful place in my being. I stood up and thanked him. He nodded, his eyes twinkling even brighter with a special gaze, then he began to walk away, humming some tune. I tuned into the frogs again and felt the breeze, admiring the dancing petals and leaves. Something caught my attention, and I looked to see where Anthony was, but he seemed to vanish behind the bush.

There was something sacred in this encounter. I returned home refreshed and made a promise to myself to return to that spot in the next few days.

The next walk, I left with greater ease and a lighter heart. I had cleared the space in my schedule to take this time of mindfulness. I heard birds and tree frogs as I walked. The Cherry Tree awaited me, the blossoms still so vibrant. I sat down and breathed deeply. I expected, or should I say hoped, to see Anthony. He didn't appear, but the loving presence embraced me. I saw the blossoms dance in a unique pattern. New messages came to me. Greater clarity dawned as I thought about the symbolic natures of the Cherry Tree and the frog calling out to remind us to fully rely on God. I smiled at this angelic sense of connection and guidance— My Cherry Blossom Channel.

A few years have passed since I started getting messages from this Cherry Blossom Channel. While I never saw Anthony again, I often felt the glowing embrace. Today, I share some of these messages on the necessity and power of self-care with others.

LOVE LIFE

Just like the acronym F.R.O.G. gave us a way to remember our connection with Source and Divine flow, LOVE LIFE is a fun way to connect daily life to the art of the sacred. I found it helped me to stay centered and vital through the stressful times.

L - Look. Take time to truly see and appreciate all the elements of our lives, especially those in nature. Cherry Trees have a special symbolism and are celebrated in Japan. The Cherry Tree awakens an awareness of the energy of faith and trust. It calls us to let go of ego and recognize that there is always a cycle to life. Blossoms will fade and fall away; new life will move through the leaves and branches, yielding fruit, and then go dormant to rest and await the new cycle of life. In Japan, they celebrate Hanami. This is a festival where families and friends go to look at the Cherry Blossoms and truly appreciate the beauty and the meaning of this beautiful aspect of Creation. They celebrate the flow of life by expressing awe and appreciation for the flow-er of Divine Love and Light blossoming all around us and within us.

O - Open hearts and open minds. Understand how to connect to forgiveness. Openness requires letting go and allowing. We cannot always control everything happening. Opening to the flow and cycles in life expands our experience. Releasing what doesn't serve us makes room to receive better feeling choices and outcomes.

V - Vibrate at a rate of your heart's greatness. Vibrate at a rate of gratefulness. Everything in the Universe is vibrating according to science. The quantum world invites us to comprehend the nature of ourselves and our world as a series of frequencies emitting and interacting, creating a matrix of possibility and reality. These vibrations are light and sound and contain information to support our journey. Sound shapes our thoughts and feelings. Being mindful of our words as vibration can help us to raise the vibe. The music we enjoy, the words others speak, the words we read, and the stories we listen to all have a vibration that can either lift us up or drag us down. Tune into the vibration that helps your heart to sing.

E - Evidence. Look for evidence of well-being. What emotions flow through your daily experiences? Do we see things as good or bad? Do we need constant external validation, or can we tune in to our center and find inner peace? The phrase "cherry pick" means to choose only what you desire. The truth is, life happens. Good, bad, ugly, indifferent. Where is the sweetness? Can we taste the joys which are available to all of us? The elixir of life is connecting with awe, joy, and appreciation.

L - Listen. Ever notice that the letters in the word Listen are the same as the word Silent? In taking care of ourselves, it is important to find stillness through mindfulness and meditation. In the space of quiet, we can connect with Nature, our Angels, our guides, our inspiration in whatever forms assist us. We are never truly alone. We are all One. Divine intelligence and Divine Love flow continually for our benefit.

I - Invite Inspiration. In the busyness of our lives and all the work we feel we need to do, we must ask ourselves, do we find meaning in all this activity or are we busy just to be busy? Cultivating relationships and activities that bring value to life is key. Finding sources of inspiration and welcoming these good vibrations helps to make life a richer experience. Also, invoking a connection to the Divine by making "I Am" statements is a powerful way to create. Make inspired statements: I am healthy, I am receiving my prosperity now, I am abundant, I am peaceful, I am Loved.... As we connect to this channel, our lives match the vibration of the inspired desires, and we see the blooms unfold around us.

F - Faith. Do we experience a sense of good fortune? Can we trust that all is in Divine Order? Faith is an attitude of certainness in a belief of what is seen and unseen working together on our behalf. There are dimensions to our existence that may seem beyond our physical perception, yet our encounter with the spiritual wonders of life can be discerned by the energetic footprints they leave upon our hearts.

E - Embrace. Embracing life with recognition that all around us is healing energy makes the experience of life juicier. There is sweetness in receiving the abounding vibration of well-being evidenced in all the ways we touch life. Like the songs of Nature, our hearts and souls commune with a divine symphony, each being a note expressing the elegance of Creation as sacred song.

Love Life… Extract the elixir of well-being by making time for self-care. The present times demand it, and our future humanity craves it.

These messages are gifts from the Cherry Blossom Channel. My intentional time in this sacred space connected me to a guidance system that supported me through the difficult days and enhanced my brighter days. My deepest hope is that you too will find the channel that speaks to your heart and gives you daily opportunities to cultivate well-being, appreciate the beauty of nature, and taste the sweetness of life.

ABOUT THE AUTHOR: Robin is a renaissance style woman being an artist, author, gardener, Reiki Master-Teacher, entrepreneur, inspirational speaker, and retreat facilitator. As a coach and consciousness guide, she uses intuitive art, sound healing, success coaching and stress reduction to activate and empower a person's transformative process. Robin has expertise in caregiver issues, being a special needs mother, Alzheimer's daughter, and founder of the Caring Circle®, a holistic support group for caregivers. She is the founder/director of HeARTs for Autism®, a nonprofit offering creative lifestyle support for Autism families. Robin's great passion is for helping people to live vitally, creatively, and abundantly.

Robin VanHorn Schwoyer
HeARTs Wellness, Inc.
PinkHeartsWellness.com
RVSchwoyer@gmail.com

Resilient Beyond Measure
Kari Kelley

My earliest memory of showing my strength took place in the kitchen of my third foster home. I was standing with my foster mother—I can't remember her name now—and I looked up at her defiantly with my hands on my hips and stomped my foot. "I'm three!" I proclaimed loudly. My foster mother smiled and patiently explained that since it was my birthday I was now four.

A few months later I would leave that home and begin a new life with my new family. The defiant proclamations and patient explanations were over. As I sat sobbing in the backseat of the car my new daddy was driving, my new mommy turned, pointed her finger at me and hissed through clenched teeth, "You shut up all that noise." These were the first of many cruel words I would hear from her. My daddy's silence was also a form of cruelty. That was the day I understood that any expression of pain was to be done in secret.

As the days, months, and years passed I learned that I was a "stupid, ugly, half-blind child who should be grateful that anyone adopted me." I believed every word of this. I knew I was stupid because I didn't do well in school. I knew I was ugly because my teeth were crooked, my hair was unmanageable and I was nothing but legs. As for being half-blind, I had optic nerve damage from a head injury, and didn't see all that well even when I wore glasses.

The foster care and adoption systems of today are much improved from when I was part of it. Back then, birth parents were encouraged to go on with their lives and not look back. In my case, my birth mother didn't even give me a first name before leaving me in the care of social services when I was three days old. My head injury occurred nine months later while I was in the process of being adopted. I bumped my head while being shaken, then left without medical attention for about ten days. I was removed from that home and that family was never allowed to adopt another child. I now have limited eye sight and two shunts in my body. I would return to foster care until I was four. I was adopted by another abusive family that could abuse me without getting caught. The scars I bear cannot be seen with the naked eye, but they hurt just as badly.

Looking back, I see myself not as a victim, but as an extremely strong child who survived shaken baby syndrome and a head injury that could have resulted in major brain damage or even death. Later, I would also survive verbal, emotional, physical, psychological, and sexual abuse at the hands of the family that adopted me at age four. This, in addition to the challenges of living with a disability.

When I think back to these early experiences, I find it amazing that I didn't end up a drug addict, an alcoholic, or even a suicide. During my teens and twenties, I did try everything to escape, including dysfunctional relationships. I believed I was lucky if anyone wanted to be with me, so I settled for relationships that had to be kept secret because the person I was dating was ashamed to be seen with me. I found myself having relationships with people who were very insecure. I mistook their desire to spend ALL their time with me for love, rather than their fear that I would leave them. I settled for shallow relationships because I believed those with no strings attached were safer.

I turned to many different religions in an attempt to soothe my unhealed wounds, but all I learned was how to be religious. I religiously went to places of worship and meetings upon meetings. I religiously read sacred texts and books of spiritual teachings. I religiously sang hymns, gospel and stayed away from any music that was unbecoming of whatever religion I found myself practicing at any given time. I religiously rattled off memorized prayers at designated times that the religion dictated. I religiously found fault in every mistake I made until I realized that being religious was never going to give me the peace and healing I was looking for.

My childhood experiences also had me convinced that I would be a horrible mother. I remember the day I made the decision that I was never having children. I was thirteen years old and overheard my mother telling someone on the phone, "I believe Kari is going to end up pregnant any minute. She is always trying to be near some man." If people with perfect eyesight, I reasoned, couldn't see that I was hurting, how would I, with my impaired sight, be able to keep a child safe?

Then came the day when I was filled with unconditional love. I call it "The day I turned green." During a guided meditation, I was asked to visualize myself with roots growing out of my feet that connected me to the earth. As I imagined these roots I pictured this lush green nutrition flowing through these roots up into my body. I observed my entire body filling with green nutrition; every inch of me, including my hair, turned green. In my vision, I saw my green self walk up to each person who had ever hurt me and put my hands on their shoulders. As I faced them I said, "I love you, I forgive you, and I understand." I saw each one of these people heal. Their posture straightened, their head lifted, and light illuminated them. The last person that I touched was myself. I saw myself heal. When I was done with that meditation I was very clear about giving and receiving unconditional love and true forgiveness. I actually felt the love I was giving and receiving in my core—the part of me that was never affected by the abuse and neglect of the human experience.

Even though it was a visualization, my physical body experienced the feeling of unconditional love. I felt myself releasing long-held anger toward my abusers. Long ago I had decided that they were void of humanity because of their treatment of me, but now, as I envisioned myself embracing person after person, I felt a sense of peace I had not thought possible. The best part of this experience was not what I gave up, but what I gained— in offering unconditional love and forgiveness to myself, it became possible for me to offer unconditional love, forgiveness, and understanding to those who had hurt me. This resulted in a profound shift in my life. Of course, it is an ongoing process—and each time I release beliefs that no longer serve me or were never true to begin with, I am able to step into my power and request and receive the desires of my heart.

Today my life is full of joy. I have a wonderful family that includes a loving and supportive husband and children who have brought me a kind of happiness I never thought possible. If I had known the many ways that children light up a life I might have reconsidered not having my own. At any rate, the sound of little feet running down the hall too early in the morning and little giggles are what kept me going on days when I would have preferred to stay in bed and bury my head. They keep me motivated to leave a legacy that they will be proud of, which to me, includes doing whatever I can to help eradicate child abuse. My heart breaks every time I read articles or hear on the news about a child that didn't survive the abuse and/or neglect of a parent or some other caregiver. There was always someone who dropped the ball, who knew the child was in harm's way and said nothing. The chain of abuse can be broken, if only people will speak their truth. According to some statistics, sixty percent of adults have never shared their experiences of being abused as children, and this allows the cycle of hurt and pain to be passed to the next generation.

Sharing my journey was a big part of my healing, and I continue to share it in the hopes that it will uplift and encourage others as well. And this has been the greatest gift of all.

ABOUT THE AUTHOR: Kari Kelley is a writer, speaker, and vocalist deeply passionate about sharing her voice of courage and inspiration. She has been featured on a wide variety of stages, panels, radio, and TV shows across the United States. Kari is the author of "Black, Blind, and Female;" the creator, producer, and performer of her one-woman show "Somebody Else's Child;" and a contributing author to the bestselling e-book Village Pearls: Spiritual Practices to Uplift your Soul. Kari has entertained VIPs at sold-out networking events all around Northern California.

Kari Kelley
Voices of Resilience
karilkelley.com
karikelleyk2@yahoo.com
408-373-7263

From Vicious Cycle to Circle of Healing

How Energy Work Transformed My Life

Rachelle Delorey

I am living proof that it is possible to break the cycle of abuse, no matter how long it has been going on or how vicious it has become. It is possible to not only survive, but thrive.

I grew up on a farm, the seventh of ten children. My parents were "old school"—born in the early 1920s and from a strict Catholic background. My father purchased the farm when he was just eighteen. He worked hard all his life and we were expected to do the same. I don't remember much about my childhood; it passed in a blur of chores and strict discipline. When dad was angry he would make us pick our own piece of wood so he could hit us with it. Once he started he never knew when to stop, and our mother never intervened. All I wanted was for someone to hug me and tell me I was loved, but instead I heard things like, "I wish you were never born," "You are useless," and "You can't do anything right." On Sundays we would go to church and then to visit our paternal grandma, who was cheated on, abused, and abusive. She would give money to some of us and not others, and someone always left feeling rejected.

When I got to high school I joined various sports—anything to keep me out of the house. Eventually I had to go home, and the situation there was worse than ever. A lot of it centered around religion. For example, one night after chores, I was in the kitchen doing my homework and listening to music when my father yelled for me to shut everything down and come say the Rosary. I pretended not to hear. When he said it again, I yelled back that I would go when I was done with my homework. The next thing I knew, he was storming into the kitchen in a rage, yelling at me, calling me a "no good," and saying he wished I was never born. Then he wrapped his hands around my throat, choking me until I could barely breathe. That night, as I followed him out of the kitchen to say the Rosary, I vowed I would get the hell out of there.

One January, my parents commented that the world would end that year if people did not pray more. All I remember thinking is well if I am going to die, I'd better have sex; at least then maybe I would feel what love is. I was fourteen at the time. This was only the beginning of looking for love in all the wrong places.

I lived for the weekends; I would hide a change of clothes outside, something to wear when I went out with my friends. One night my parents found out I was at the bar and came to get me there. They dragged me out to the truck, where my father started pounding me on the chest for being "part of evil," for being in the "Sinful Place." I was grounded for a while but I did not care. My repeated escapes continued after my parents were asleep. I would party all night and sneak in before six a.m., plenty of time before dad woke us up at six-thirty. I also got beaten more times than I could count.

When I met my first husband, he was twenty-six years old and had already been married. When my parents heard about it, they said I was sinning with a married man and ordered me to stay away from him; if I didn't, they said, I'd be going to hell. The more they tried to keep me away from him, the more I rebelled. I no longer cared what they thought. I continued to go out, sometimes leaving on a Friday night and not coming home until Sunday.

On my sixteenth birthday, my boyfriend called and said he would pick me up and take me to see my brother in Ottawa. He didn't have to ask me twice. My parents weren't home at the time and I never bothered to phone them. When my brother told me that my parents had called the police, I hid at my boyfriend's place for two weeks. The cops were indeed looking for me. They knocked until we answered the door and when they questioned me I told them I had been beaten at home. Because I was sixteen they told me to just stay out of trouble or they would take me back to my parents.

In 1976, one year after I graduated high school, we married. A child followed, but my husband was too busy partying and doing drugs to help. I always felt so lonely, abandoned, dejected, not wanted or needed. A few months after our second child was born he left with a stripper, and I moved with the children to British Columbia to start over.

My second marriage brought with it a large blended family; my new husband and I had five children between us, ranging from two to nine years old. This, however, was the least of our challenges. My husband hated his stressful job, and often came home angry, blaming me for everything. I could do nothing right—he would tell me I was way too fat to be his wife, then berate me if I didn't eat. When he couldn't get to me, he verbally and emotionally abused the children, especially mine. I left him for four years and went back home after the kids had all moved out, hoping that things would change. It was good for four or five months, then the mental and emotional abuse started with more intensity. I cried all day, went to work, and was bullied there, then came home and got it again. I started leaving the house at six in the morning and staying out until eleven at night. This vicious cycle continued until one night in September of 2007, when I went to my first Reiki Circle.

When I walked into the room, I had no idea what to expect; I just knew I needed...something. As we shared and received healing, I realized it was the first time I'd felt real love and acceptance. When I left that night it was like a thousand pounds had been released from me and I knew I had something to learn. Just two weeks later, I told my husband I was leaving for good. I also resigned from my job where I was bullied, and since then I have been self-employed, living my passion through Holistic Healing. I started with learning Reiki so I could teach and assist others in identifying their root issues so they could release and heal their life.

I was on my own for five years. In that time, I attended workshops and took courses in Reiki Level I to Grand Master, Healing Touch, Healing Pathways, Thought Field Therapy, Matrix Energetics, The Emotion Code, The Body Code, Anatomy, Physiology and Modalities, Physics and Spiritual Healing for

Healers. I learned to love myself and release much of the trauma I had been carrying around since childhood.

There was just one area in which I was still vulnerable, and that was relationships. A man I met through a social media site scammed me out of thousands of dollars and I had to declare bankruptcy. Sometime later, a friend convinced me—against my better judgment—to join a dating site. Within a few days I was introduced to a man and decided to overlook the many red flags I saw. When eight months later he asked me to move in with him, I was both excited and scared. I gave myself completely to him and in my heart I hoped I would be with him forever. I spent the next four years ignoring his lies, deceptions, and many addictions. The straw that broke the camel's back was a phone call I accidentally intercepted. He had decided, without any regard for what I might want, to sell our home and move to Vancouver Island. He would go ahead without me, and he said I could join him later on. Throughout our relationship everything had to be his way, and this was no different. That phone call, however, revealed his true intentions: he had gone to the Island, not only to pursue part-time work, but to meet other women. He wanted to have me at home and still be free to do what he wanted with whomever he wanted.

After that, I knew our relationship was over. But there was an upside; he had introduced me to amazing friends who helped me through the last three years with him, allowing me to cry on their shoulders. In the end, though, I had to be the one to decide I would not let people walk all over me anymore. I would no longer let another human being destroy me, disrespect me, or abuse me. I'd had enough of feeling like a victim; it was time to break the patterns of self-destructive behavior and lack of self-love, not only for myself but for my family members that were following my footsteps. I made the decision to end this abuse.

Another pivotal point happened when I was cracked wide open from this relationship. I went on a two-week intensive training on Vancouver Island, where I learned The Black Pearl Technique, CCMBA—Complete Memory Body Alignment, and thirty-plus techniques to release trauma from my life. For the first week, I cried intensely, but as days passed, deep healing began to occur. I cleared multi-generational patterns of abuse, which transformed and metamorphosed my relationships with everyone; I learned to heal my inner child, and about the trigger points in our bodies that allow us to release all emotional energy centers of the body. Some of the healing and releasing was done by hypnosis. By using muscle testing we connect to the subconscious, which remembers ninety-five percent of everything that has happened to us, not only in this life but in previous incarnations as well. Now I teach others how to heal from the past and live a brighter future. On my website it shows all the modalities and techniques I have learned and I share my knowledge with others.

The Emotion Code and Body Code were extremely crucial on my healing journey. It is an energy healing technique that helps us identify and release trapped emotions that stem from past events. Having my heart wall removed also helped in connecting with others and lifted bouts of depression and anxiety. Trapped emotions are made of energy, just like our body, and they exert an influence on the physical tissues and even cause pain. Releasing trapped emotions created the right condition for my body to heal. My physical and emotional difficulties disappeared, and I was able to live a more authentic life without the baggage I'd been carrying around. It also released emotions from ancestors and their descendants, alive or dead.

Many years ago, I found out that my dad had been physically, verbally, and emotionally abused by his own father and many other relatives. My dad has since passed, and I forgave him many years ago, knowing he did the best he could, given his own experiences, to raise us. I am grateful for the harsh life lessons I learned, as it made me a stronger person.

Today I am no longer the little meek female, but a powerful female warrior. I have set my boundaries and people are testing me. I chose to live to the fullest, with joy, compassion, and gratitude for the teachers (partners) that helped crack me wide open so light could come in and I could stand up for myself. I still do daily healings on myself; it all starts with self-love, self-worth, self-esteem, and rebuilding from the inside. Just like on an airplane we put on our mask first before we can put it on someone else.

Forgiveness is crucial and the most important first step to heal thyself. True love can only come from within no one can give you what you need, except yourself.

ABOUT THE AUTHOR: Rachelle Delorey is a certified Reiki Grand Master Teacher and Certified Emotion Code and Body Code Practitioner. She practices The Balance Procedure and more than thirty other modalities and techniques to facilitate healing for herself and her clients—human and animal. Her own journey to wholeness began ten years ago after going to her first Reiki Circle, and now she lives her passion by teaching others how to fulfill their wellness goals: mental, physical, emotional, and spiritual. Rachelle is the mother of five grown children and has thirteen grandchildren. She loves reading, writing poetry, gardening, and being in nature.

Rachelle Alice Delorey
Perpetual Transformation of the Body, Mind, and Soul
perpetualtransformation.ca
rachelle@perpetualtransformation.ca
250-961-0714

Healing Through Purpose
Nikki Maly

Ever since I was a child, I've had a gut feeling or "knowing" about people or situations, an inner voice that would alert me if something wasn't right. Sometimes it was a peculiar feeling in my stomach when I was doing something I later would be reprimanded for by my parents; on other, more serious occasions, the word *danger* would flash strongly in my mind, accompanied by a hair-raising sensation. I listened and it kept me out of harm's way. But somewhere along the line, I seemed to have lost it or lost touch with it. It was like trying to navigate life with no compass, and by my early twenties I found myself overweight, hopeless, and deeply unhappy, with no sense of who I was or how to move forward. Like a puzzle piece in the wrong box, I didn't seem to fit, and every attempt I made to improve my life seemed to be shut down before it began. When I couldn't find fulfillment with the outside world, I turned inward to search for happiness and purpose. For the next few years I made it a point to read something uplifting each day; I also diligently wrote my own thoughts daily. Both practices brought me tremendous insights.

Against the opinions of others and with all the courage I could muster, I left my six-year relationship and the home we shared. Though it was the right choice, it brought with it financial challenges. I worked two different shift jobs and still struggled to pay the bills. It was as if the life was being sucked out of me. By the time I was evicted from my apartment several months later, I was mentally, physically, and spiritually exhausted. I had lost everything I worked so hard for since the break-up, and I was unsure where to turn. It was then that my gut feeling returned, and I decided to follow it.

A few months earlier, my estranged grandfather had asked me

if I wanted to come stay with him. I had declined at the time, but now I called and asked if the offer was still available. Thankfully, he said yes, and before I knew it, I was on a plane for sunny Florida. It was a leap of faith to be sure, but I intuitively knew it was the right decision, even though it was against my mother's wishes and I feared she might disown me because of it. During the flight, I made a decision to embrace the unknown, reconnect with the family I hadn't seen since childhood, and hopefully fill the emptiness in my heart.

In Florida, I found myself surrounded by people who looked like me and sometimes acted like me too. Lifelong habits were explained, including food cravings, because I used to eat those foods as a kid. For the first time I felt as though I understood myself. The risks had been worth it, and life was finally starting to make sense.

Still, there was something missing. I had a good job, healed some old wounds, and was living in the state I loved, but I lacked purpose. This proved to be a destructive force in my life. Against my better judgment (intuition), I found myself hanging around the wrong types of people and dealing with the kind of troubles that come with bad company. I knew I was better than the choices I was making, but that hole in my heart was still there and I was desperate to fill it with something, anything. Eventually, I fell into a deep, dark depression. I often missed work, and sometimes didn't even get out of bed to eat or bathe. On "good" days, I would return home from work and head right back to bed. My failure to thrive was evident just by looking at me—I had become very thin, with bags under my eyes and dull, lifeless skin. In fact, my whole life was dull and lifeless. This couldn't be all there was for me, I knew something had to change.

I prayed for God to step in. I knew I didn't come this far *just* to come this far! I reignited the fighter in me and searched again for what inspired my heart. I kept my mind open for the right answer and tried a couple different religions to see if one called to me.

Then one day a friend suggested I see a woman he knew—she was a psychic and according to him a very good one. Though I knew my parents would most certainly not approve, I scheduled an appointment in the hopes that she'd help guide me in the right direction. I figured if her advice didn't feel right I would dismiss it, but her reading proved to be accurate, and her advice confirmed my own intuition. I continued to meet with her, and in time she introduced me to a healing modality called Reiki. When I received my first attunement through her, I wasn't even sure it had done anything for me. I just knew it felt good to learn about this new healing. Looking back, I truly believe it made everything that followed possible.

A short time later I overheard a coworker talking about his experience with yoga. At the time I thought nothing of it, but I soon found that yoga kept creeping into my thoughts. Finally, I took notice and sought out a class. I distinctly remember looking at the clock five minutes before class and thinking, *What the heck am I doing here? I haven't the slightest idea of what we are about to do.* I listened to my heart, overcame my anxiety, and stayed. Soon yoga was a regular part of my routine. I had also found subliminal mediations involving Theta brainwaves created a positive impact on my days. Around the same time, the psychic, who had become a good friend, recommended a class on how to access Theta on your own. Although I was reluctant at first, I took notice of the feeling in my heart and signed up. The ThetaHealing® class reminded me how powerful my intuition was and taught me that there was a way to strengthen this skill. The key was to pick up on the subtle clues I received and note the signs that my intuition's strength was growing. It became like a game, and the more I noticed the more I received.

I started with small requests, things that didn't make a difference whether it came to manifestation or not; for example, I would set an intention to find a close parking spot or ask my angels to find me a sale on something I needed; then I would release the thought and any attachment to it like a balloon into the sky. When my requests were fulfilled, I gave thanks to Creator, my guides, and angels for their guidance and help. This became a daily routine and with regular use my abilities grew and expanded, like a flower budding and then into bloom. In the process, I continued to heal a little more of myself too. Life started to open for me in unexpected ways. I received a promotion and started building relationships with my coworkers. I found work to be fulfilling, which gave me a sense of purpose. Physically I felt better too, thanks to the many benefits yoga brought into my life.

I really thought I had "arrived," especially when I applied for a position within my company and was picked over two-hundred other applicants! Brimming with excitement, I signed up for the next ThetaHealing class. I was eager to learn more about using and trusting my intuition.

Shortly after taking that class, I received more excellent news: my teacher wanted me to work as her assistant in exchange for more classes! At my "real job," however, my victory was short-lived. The pressure and demands, coupled with turbulent relationships with my manager and team, were weighing heavily on me. I was losing my confidence and the quality of my work suffered as a result. I felt as if I had slipped into a parallel universe where nothing went right. How could my career take a one-hundred-eight-degree turn in such a short time? I struggled to understand the purpose of this latest challenge.

I frequently found myself reaching out to my teacher and classmates for support, and using the techniques taught in class, sessions with friends, and yoga as an escape; in fact, ThetaHealing and yoga had become my top priorities. Eventually, I realized that the troubles at work were a catalyst for using my intuition and finding my purpose, and I was able to move out of that role, grateful for the experience. Without the intense push I'm not sure I would have dived headfirst into my new lifestyle. Within two years I had taken all the classes my teacher had to offer. As a result my intuition was fierce, I had acquired more intuitive abilities and I found a support group of wonderful loving friends.

After the realization that using my intuition and my passion for helping others was my path, I signed up for ThetaHealing instructor's training and became a Reiki Master in the same year. Afterward, as an informal graduation gift for these accomplishments and years of training, my teacher asked me to accompany her at an ashram in the Bahamas as her assistant for a class. It was a magical experience and a beautiful way to celebrate my new endeavors. At first there were some frustrations. Completely out of my element, I had a crash course in Hindu culture. We woke up at 5:30 each morning to meditate and then chant in Sanskrit to the rising sun. This was certainly a challenge— I wasn't sure how to read Sanskrit, let alone say the long words on the page! Before long I found these songs ringing in my head even days after I returned. I had the honor of being a part of a *puja*, which is a spiritual ceremony involving a Hindu priest at the beginning and close of the class. All of this happened against a tropical backdrop and the sound of the ocean nearby. To this day, whenever I light a specific incense I am reminded of that adventure and how far I have come.

Listening to my intuition and my heart, and not the opinions of those around me, is what took me from the passenger seat and into the driver's seat of my life. Both yoga and ThetaHealing have made such a monumental impact on my life; I can't mention one without acknowledging the other because the two are the foundation of my spiritual practice. ThetaHealing empowered me with the ability and knowledge that everything I've ever needed was already inside of me, just waiting to be liberated. It gave me the opportunity to obtain my heart's desires. My yoga practice gave me a safe place to get out of my head and center myself again. I also recognized that yoga quieted the monkey mind, which gave my intuition a chance to shine and provided clarity on several tough situations. Each time I got knocked down or felt like everything had fallen apart, I got back up, brushed myself off, and returned to my spiritual practice for answers and guidance. I then found my life came back together better than before and drew me even closer to achieving my goals. With the use of my spiritual practice I built a confidence and tenacity unlike before.

Now, I'm eager to share my spiritual gifts with all those who are open and willing. Teaching others the instruments that transformed my life is my gift to bestow to the world. One of my greatest joys is to witness my student's growth from the beginning to end of the first ThetaHealing class. Their evolution is drastic and to watch them discover themselves in a way they never thought possible is always uplifting and enormously rewarding as a teacher. Through the various ups and downs, twists and turns I am grateful for all lessons learned, the profound healing I experienced, and the amazing souls I've been blessed to encounter along the way.

ABOUT THE AUTHOR: Nikki Maly is an Intuitive Specialist, yoga instructor and alchemist dedicated to supporting all those seeking healing, life transformation, and self-empowerment. Trained in the healing arts of Usui Reiki, ThetaHealing and Hatha Yoga, she combines these techniques with her intuition and her connection to her guides to illuminate the divine spark that already lives within her clients and students. Nikki lives and works in Orlando, Florida; however, because energy is not restricted by distance, she provides healing sessions and intuitive consultations to clients abroad by phone or Skype. She also travels to teach students the techniques that transformed her life.

Nikki Maly
Intuitive Illumination
Intuitiveillumination.com
Intuitiveillumination@gmail.com
407-883-6852

The Messages in Our Bottles: Transforming Pain into Freedom

Jackie Rioux

I am often asked why I do what I do and how I got to this place in my life—a place of love, purpose, and passion. The answer is not a short one, for my journey has been an incredible adventure of learning, synchronicities, and epiphanies. There has also been plenty of trauma, but I am here to say that your worst trauma is often your greatest gift towards—and the key to—your life purpose. Why else would we go through such hardships, but to learn life lessons and build character? My legacy is to share my journey with others, to be an inspiration and encouragement whenever I can. I am my own walking testimony.

I grew up in Northern British Columbia, Canada, in the area where the Great Spirit Bear Kermode lives. On road trips to visit my grandmother we passed through my birth town of Smithers, BC. My mother would point to the mountaintop forestry lookout tower where my father used to work and where I was conceived (I love to tease her about that now). Perhaps this is where my love of mountains comes from. According to Akashic records, this aspect of my conception is indicative that I am one of eight-hundred special souls who have come to Earth to encourage others. It didn't always feel this way, however. Although I do have good memories, most of my early life was overshadowed with trauma, upsets, and a myriad of fears. We often had boarders and foster kids living with us. When I was six, a certain sixteen-year-old boy stayed with us for the summer. The sexual abuse—and his subsequent threats to torture me and kill my parents if I told anyone—left me with deep fears of darkness, guns, confined spaces, heights, being alone in the forest, and being tied up. I also had trust issues, a multitude of "triggers", and recurring nightmares well into my twenties. I had a skewed sense of respectable personal and social boundaries as well. This, however, was only the first of four separate cases of childhood sexual abuse I would endure before the age of fourteen. My father had a totalitarian rule over our home. I was his confidante, "Daddy's girl", and he took his "teaching" with me across a line a father should never cross. This in turn damaged my relationship with my mother.

These experiences and the resulting shame and low self-esteem contributed to many years of being bullied and withdrawn throughout my grade school years. When I was fifteen, I latched on to the first boy who told me I was beautiful. Ironically, he had been one of the boys who picked on me back in grade six. Thinking I could escape my father, I got pregnant right away, but I had only jumped from frying pan into the fire. My new husband was rarely home, and when he was home he had an unpredictable volatile temper. It was a tumultuous relationship, exacerbated by my childhood secrets that had surfaced, and at one point he slit his wrists while I was at home.

He was also unable to hold a steady job, and our time on social assistance ended only after I secured a job at the post office. With my new income security, I was able to help him secure a business loan, which he used to buy a carpet cleaning business. That venture was productive for a while, but my husband lacked business sense and it eventually became a financial strain. Our marriage was stagnant as well. It takes two to make it work, and after a total of four children and ten years, I gave up. The truth was, we were both mentally immature and contributed to the breakdown. There were several years of tearful conflict in court over maintenance and custody as he blamed me for everything, and left me with the majority of the marriage and business debt. At twenty-eight I found myself divorced with four children to raise. I would learn many harsh life lessons during that time, lessons that most people learn in their teenage years. For all I had been through, I was in many ways extremely naïve. My childhood issues lurked beneath the surface, and I attracted all the wrong people into my life. I have been lied to, betrayed, violated and heartbroken more times than I care to count.

In 2002, a whirlwind romance and impromptu marriage turned into a two-year nightmare with a pathological liar. Whereas my first husband's neglect had brought out my abandonment issues, my second husband's clinginess amplified my claustrophobia issues. When I finally said I wanted a divorce, he overdosed on prescription pills and had a seizure in front of me. When one marriage fails, it is easy to blame the other person. When a second marriage fails, it is time to look in the mirror! I was so scarred from that marriage that I didn't date anyone for almost six years. It was a lonely time of my life, yet it was also when my personal growth accelerated, and since then I have learned to enjoy my own company, rather than relying on a romantic partner.

As children go through the various stages of development, they often assert their independence by throwing tantrums until they learn healthy coping skills with which to navigate the world. I believe this process is not limited to children and that we go through these growth stages at any point in life. That said, it is more difficult to learn these skills as an adult, when we are "expected" to be mature. Trauma keeps us stuck in the past and creates a landmine of unresolved triggers. For some, these triggers cause an explosion of rage; I, on the other hand, would implode, withdrawing into myself like a wounded animal. I have since learned my issues were similar to hypo-sexuality and PTSD, and this manifested in my early life as poor choices and coping skills.

Childhood sexual abuse ravages a person on every level, right down to the core of their being. It can manifest physically and be a precursor to internal health issues. Twice in my life I went through the horrifying experience of passing a kidney stone. The pain was so excruciating, I would rather go through all four of my childbirth labors at once than ever go through that again. In 2006, I had been sick for over a year with stomach issues for which my doctor could not find a reason. I had unexpected flare-ups, often while out on my mail route and I took excessive sick leave that year. Eventually my doctor discovered that I had an ulcer. This was also unbearably painful, and there were times I wondered if this is what it is like to die. Between my illness and disruptive office politics at work, coupled with yet another court battle with my ex-husband, I was overwhelmed. On April 23, 2008, I reached my breaking point. While at work I erupted in hives and began hyperventilating. Realizing something had to be done, I took three months off work and re-evaluated my life. I knew I couldn't stay in a job that was no longer aligned with my values, and the other areas of my life were not going well either.

Not long after my soul-searching began, I started experiencing a series of synchronistic events that would change my life. First, with this new perspective, I enrolled in an evening Psych 101 class. I had always been interested in psychology, but with my financial and time constraints, I had never before been able to pursue it. Within just a few exhilarating and intriguing classes, I knew I had found my happy place. Around this time, I met a lady who was involved in a women's business network. She introduced me to a line of nutrition products that helped heal my stomach. Later, I also met several influential mentors, teachers, and business people who catapulted my personal growth to new levels. I took classes and courses, learned new skills, and started my own business, Ladybug Wellness. The ulcer experience had turned out to be a blessing in disguise. The breakdown at work was the pivotal point that changed my life path and my healing journey. I am grateful for the corporate job that provided a steady income so that I could raise my children, but after twenty-six years, it was time to go. My decision to explore other avenues allowed me to retire early and focus solely on my passion.

Through the years, counseling was a source of support, but not relief. I was numb, yet easily triggered. At one point, as a therapeutic release, I wrote out my disturbing ordeals in detail. There is an analogy I like to use about trauma. Each event is like a ship in a glass bottle. Each time an upsetting event happens, we put the pieces together in the bottle and place it on a shelf. Whenever a new upset happens, those glass bottles fall and shatter on the floor and we seem to relive everything all over again. Over time we get more efficient at putting everything into glass bottles and putting them back on the shelf, but they are always there and always fragile. When we begin our real healing journey, we start to put those pieces back into Plexiglas bottles, and eventually we can close the door on the storage room that holds those bottles. There are no longer any triggers that pull us into the oblivion of glass shards, compounded pain, and an overwhelming disorganized mess.

The most profound transformation came when I was introduced to The Emotion Code, a non-invasive technique adept in releasing the emotional charge that keeps us rooted in traumatic thoughts and blind to the good memories. I was finally able to put those horrific memories in the past where they belong! These days, the writings of my ordeals now read like someone else's story. I can remember those events if I choose to, but they are not in the forefront of my mind anymore. The wonderful memories have now been unblocked and my future looks brighter as well. I can feel—and am grateful for—all the good things in my life!

Music is the language of the soul and has always been a source of inspiration throughout various times of my life. The various genres from metal to instrumental classics have been indicative of the themes of my life; from rebellion and anger, sorrow and loss, to contemplation and happiness. I am grateful for the many activities that have helped me gain confidence over the years, including modeling, Toastmasters, hiking, scuba diving, firearms safety courses, and skydiving. Most of all, I am grateful for my maternal grandmother's Christian influence in my life. Faith has been my solace.

My relationships have also healed. My father passed in 2014. Our relationship was contentious, but thankfully I learned to forgive him for the past before that point. He raised me with his own continued cycle of abuse. No matter the relationship with our parents, when they are gone, we grieve. And I cried profusely. It was from him that I gained my love of rocks and nature, my resourceful survival skills, and my fascination with words and language. As the eldest of four girls, he was hard on me; but that adversity is part of what forged my inner strengths. My relationship with my mother has also drastically improved and I am blessed to have many wonderful friends as well.

The bio-energetic modalities and techniques I use have allowed me to witness miracles of transformation in myself, my loved ones, and my clients. My worst trauma has emerged as my gift of compassion and encouragement, and I share these resources with others through my website to assist them with their personal growth. When asked about my philosophy on life, I defer to Bon Jovi: "Take my hand, we'll make it I swear, Livin' on a Prayer."

ABOUT THE AUTHOR: Jackie lives in Prince George BC Canada. She has four grown children and four grandchildren, so far. She retired from an exhausting corporate job in June 2016 and now lives her passion through encouraging and empowering others to find their own life purpose by overcoming trauma and letting go of the past. Jackie is a practitioner in several bio-energetic modalities and techniques. She is a perpetual student, always eager to progress in personal growth. With her interest in human nature and psychology, she shares her extensive list of resources and tidbits of wisdom on her website at www.ladybugwellness.ca

Jackie Rioux
Ladybug Wellness
ladybugwellness.ca
jackie@ladybugwellness.ca
250-961-6190

Life is Beautiful
Angela Hanna

Life is beautiful, and every moment of it precious. I know this to the core of my being…now. But that was not how I felt as I slowly regained consciousness in a hospital bed that Friday night in 2011. In fact, I was horrified to be alive. For despite my best efforts, I was not meant to die that day; it would seem that God had other plans for me, although what those were, I had no idea. I was exhausted, empty, and could not see a path in life for myself past this day. The date—April 1st—was another cruel irony. It seemed the April Fools' joke was on me.

That very morning I had stood at my kitchen window and watched the birds frolicking. They chirped happily under a clear blue sun-drenched sky. I felt the fresh spring breeze on my face and tried to take a deep breath. What should have woken and stirred my senses with the exciting promise of new beginnings left me just as it had found me, hollow inside. The winter, so cold and dark, had smothered the life inside me. I was numb; there were no more tears to cry and I could feel absolutely nothing. I remember experiencing something within me disconnect as I went back to sleep that morning with the desperate hope I would not wake.

As far back as I can remember my mother had told me that it was only through selfless service and sacrifice that I would experience happiness and fulfillment. Although both my parents had hearts like lions in the way of generosity and hospitality, they were very demanding of their children.

Mom had to work to make ends meet, which meant I was given the responsibility for my younger sister. In addition to my regular household chores, I walked her to school every day and walked her home for lunch; then after preparing the meal and cleaning up, we'd head back to school for the afternoon. It was as if I had become a mother at the tender age of nine.

The hardest part of shouldering these duties was the expectation of perfection. If things were not done just right, I was shamed and humiliated. If at any time during this process I happened to speak up in my own defense, physical punishment followed.

The slightest deviation from my mother's instruction would be seen by her as a lack of appreciation, gratitude, and respect on my part. After a while, I stopped defending myself. I wanted so very much to be loved and I was willing to do anything to meet the requirements. A program was set in place for me right there and then, and it went something like this: I had to be obedient, smart, hardworking, supportive, responsible, conscientious, and self-sacrificing. I had no other recourse; I had to be the best at everything because only then I would be worthy of being loved.

I became a people pleaser in every way possible. I was a successful student, a kind and loving daughter, and eventually a supportive wife and a fiercely dedicated mother. I measured my own self-worth by how much I gave to others. The happier I could make them, the more I could justify my very existence. I had no idea how ingrained this false belief had become, or the destruction it would inflict on my life.

As an adult my identity revolved around my devotion to my husband and kids, much as it had my nuclear family during my childhood. When our firstborn, a beautiful little girl, passed away after eighteen months, I blamed myself and wondered what I could have done differently. Guilt was familiar to me and so I visited often. Our second son was diagnosed as special needs at age five, and at that point I started to believe that I must have angered God, but how? I was trying so hard to be perfect!

Despite my hidden and sometimes not-so-hidden grief, our home was always sparkling clean. I cooked five-star meals and my sole focus was to make sure my family was happy. I could not pursue even part-time work outside the home because my son needed so much of my attention. The isolation and feelings of being trapped were intolerable. Here I was, a college graduate and completely financially dependent on my husband. The truth was, we were both stuck in roles we were not comfortable with.

Over time, the more I gave of myself, the more invisible I

became. I was disappearing from my own life. My body and mind were profoundly depleted, but it barely registered. Being unloved or unlovable was a fate worse than death to me.

Bouts of anxiety and depression would completely overtake me. Even during those periods of profound loneliness and mental detachment I tried my best to seem "functional." Life buzzed around me, but I was frozen.

When this façade no longer worked, I screamed, cursed, and blamed everything and everyone for not being sensitive to my needs. But If I didn't know what I needed, how could anyone else?

I finally stopped talking entirely. This was the beginning of the deepest darkest night for my soul, which ultimately culminated in an attempt to escape this world.

But even that would not go my way.

August of that year ushered in a milestone birthday for me and I decided to take a trip to celebrate it, alone. This would be a time of contemplation and self-discovery. I went to an island so remote that it could only be reached first by airliner, then a tiny ten-passenger plane and a ferry. There, I had a life changing experience that altered the trajectory of my life.

I brought two books with me. The first was a journal to record my thoughts, feelings, and experiences; the second was Dr. Bradley Nelson's "The Emotion Code," which I had found "randomly," or so I thought. I am now a true believer that there are no accidents, everything happens for a reason. Back then, all I knew was that I was drawn to the cover.

I carried this book with me everywhere, often wiping tears away as I read. It seemed as if Dr. Bradley was writing about me. He explained how trapped emotions from difficult experiences—as well as those inherited and absorbed while in utero, can and often do negatively impact our lives. All this baggage keeps us stuck in negative patterns that often attract more pain and suffering and keep us away from attaining our full potential.

He also wrote about the "Heart Wall" and how having one can stop us from healing on a physical level and how it altered our ability to give and receive love, leaving us feeling numb.

A few pages in, I was hooked and soon began practicing muscle testing.

This tiny island was heaven on earth, a true paradise. Time flowed as slow as molasses and as I reveled only in the present moment, magic began happening.

After settling in for a day or two, I had the urge to explore. Bikes were provided so I went for leisurely rides.

On one adventure I found a little path through a brush and turned onto it. I had no idea where I was going or what I would find, but it didn't matter—my curiosity had gotten the better of me. A few minutes later I cleared the brush and saw before me the most incredible sight. It was a deserted beach—and one of the most spectacular seascapes I had ever seen—untouched, pure and teeming with sea creatures. There were crabs, birds, turtle eggs that I helped rebury in the sand. The ocean was powerful, the breeze seemed to speak to me and joy filled my heart. The beauty alone brought me to a state of awe and reverence. I just couldn't help but give thanks to God for the splendor that was laid out before me. I felt like I had been called to a sacred experience. There was NOBODY there. It was meant to be; I was granted the grace of having it all to myself. It was out of the way for a reason, so only seekers would find it. It had always existed but I would have never known how profoundly it would change me until I took the chance and the time to go inward.

On that pivotal day I stood with my arms outstretched and my eyes turned up towards the bluest, clearest sky, tears covered my face as I opened my heart fully to God and allowed healing to take place. All the while that powerful Atlantic salty ocean breeze seemed to penetrate every cell in my body. At that very moment, I felt as though I had finally connected to my spirit. Something had shifted and everything changed, just as even the slightest turn of the kaleidoscope changes the entire picture. I had been infused with a love so profound and overwhelming that it could only be described as sacred. I fell to my knees with gratitude.

On that beach I had my first calling but that was a conversation with the Creator that I hold too dear to discuss. What I can share with you is that I was given a message. I was to share this love and healing with the world and that I would never be alone.

In the spring of 2012 I attended my first Emotion Code seminar. It was there that I purchased The Body Code Modality and began using it on myself. The more blocks and imbalances I cleared, the more clarity I had.

If The Emotion Code was a cool refreshing drink to my thirsty soul, The Body Code was the whole meal, the nourishment that gave me hope, strength and the courage I needed to make new beginnings. These modalities saved my life and opened up my awareness and my heart to new exciting possibilities. I was free from those constraining beliefs and programs that had suffocated me all those years. I experienced a peacefulness I had never known. I began Certification for The Emotion Code on November 19, 2012 and became certified on March 26, 2013. In June of the same year I began certification for The Body Code and received my full certification on December 4, 2013.

I now do this work full time. It is my passion. Now I help others, not because it is tied to my own self-worth, but simply because I found my joy and wish the same for all my clients. Whether they are suffering physically or emotionally, as I was, The Body Code gets to the root of the challenge.

I have seen physical pain, some of which had been chronic and long-standing, completely resolved, and even cancerous tumors reduced in size. Emotional challenges like depression, PTSD, and Anxiety, as well as Tourette's syndrome profoundly reduced. Reproductive issues, from absent menses to infertility, were resolved. Blocks to love, abundance, and money were released. As a result some of my clients have doubled or even tripled their income through diverse streams. I have had the pleasure of working with so many children and grandchildren of all ages, helping them to navigate this big world with as little baggage as possible. I have successfully worked with pets, some with severe challenges.

Finally, I feel grateful for even the darkest of times in my life, since without them I am not sure that I would have the degree of compassion I have for my own clients.

I am blessed. Yes indeed, life is beautiful, and every moment of it precious!

ABOUT THE AUTHOR: Angela has been "sensitive" for as long as she can remember; however, all her gifts came flooding in only a few years back. By what she could only describe as grace, she was shown that her past, painful life experiences were to be used to help others. Since then she has worked full time with people of all ages and animals of all kinds from the four corners of the earth. Using primarily The Emotion and Body Code modalities, she works to free them from emotional and physical limitations so they can live the very best version of their lives. Angela's clients describe her as being highly intuitive, divinely guided, and deeply compassionate.

Angela Hanna, CECP, CBCP, D.PSc
Integrated Energy Wellness
Integratedenergywellness.com
angela@integratedenergywellness.com
514-894-2351

The Journey of Full Circle
Carly Alyssa Thorne

Think of the title of this book collaboration, *Heal Thy Self.* I want you to truly see the word *SELF.* This is what my chapter is about, the journey and circle of being in our wounds, our cycles, finding our strength to choose to get the mentors and help we need. Discovering our *ahas* and then becoming the victors and warriors we are, and then choosing compassion, integrity and helping others, not with a hand-out, yet with a hand up so they can find their way out of the maze we were once in.

Some of you may know my story, others will not. It's a long one, so I'll give you broad strokes to get the points across, while sharing enough so you see the patterns and hopefully discover your own ahas.

My birth initials—S.O.S. —were appropriate. Growing up with severe sexual, verbal, and physical abuse, and many health challenges, in a dysfunctional household, I was certainly in distress! I left the United States at the age of five and returned at the age of fourteen after traveling and living in Mexico, Venezuela, and Brazil. As a child, moving, changing schools often, being the new girl, having all the secrets, having parents that traveled often, et cetera—you get the picture—it was very difficult and lonely.

When I was young I was extremely angry on the inside and feisty on the outside; I was also very quiet, small, and invisible when I needed to be. I exhibited the traits of what they used to call being the "wallflower" or the product of abuse and showing the signs of a survivor. Today, I don't use terms like survivor, victim et cetera; I use words like victor, thriver, and warrior, and I will explain this further as we explore the journey of the circle and self.

The circle, ah, how does that work? We do what we do based on what we know unconsciously, even though we may grow up saying I will never, ever marry or do what my brother, mother, father, environment, experiences, et cetera, taught me. So what did I do…?

My Journey and Circle of Life

First Marriage

A man I loved who never hit me or yelled at me, and I LOVED his family. They raised me, after all, took me in, loved me for who I was, and I didn't want to lose them, I even moved in with them. I didn't care he was JUST an alcoholic who fought with me over the keys every weekend, and drank every night. That was okay, right? Eventually I couldn't take it anymore and left; however, I never truly resolved things. I was always just a bulldozer; I just walked away from things. I did remain very close to his family, by the way, just not him.

Second Marriage

A nice Jewish man who was from the city; around the same age as me; not into drugs and a social drinker; and a family that seemed nice. I was running a New Age pre-school out of my home called "Learning, Playing, and Growing, Inc." and he was in the entertainment business, so I thought all would be well. Long story short, old patterns of behaviors began to appear: he hates commuting from the suburbs to New York City each day; he starts to resent the life created in the suburbs, et cetera. His behavior drastically changes and he starts to take it out on me. He moves back to NYC.

Third Marriage

The cycle continues and the ante goes up. His family was great, close knit, with women who got together and canned fruits and vegetables and played cards every week. I *loved the family.*

Hmm…are we noticing a pattern yet? Husband was a corrections officer at a prison, with a close group of friends who all worked at the same places and all loved to hunt. Problem: they would all work double shifts so they could then go hunting, so basically the wives were hunting widows who were left to care for their children, or in my case, left with his family, and if I dared say anything, the verbal abuse and other old familiar patterns I knew too well would begin.

Most people would say—in fact, they have said—that I am crazy and I shouldn't have married this many times. However, in my mind it made sense. I wasn't into one-night stands or just living with people; I believed if you were going to be with someone for more than a year or two, you get married. So, here we are, nearing the end of an era of abuse; and I finally started standing up for myself, discovering my patterns, and divorcing all who choose to not believe in me and call me a liar, et cetera...and I got the help I needed and made a life decision to choose me. I also made a choice to stand up for others; take responsibility for my part in life; let go of all things no longer serving me and take the leap—regardless of what others thought—and fly.

Fourth Marriage

Finally, the straw that broke the camel's back and completed the cycle. The fate that literally saved my life and for which I am forever grateful. He'd worked for the same company for eighteen years; was allergic to alcohol, and didn't do drugs when I first met him; and had a *close-knit family,* whom I loved. Then he got hurt on the job. Painkillers became his friend and the rollercoaster began. My life was no longer safe; my life became my past from start to finish, and each day I had to choose between life and death. I literally never knew when I went to sleep whether I would wake up the next day. The mantra I heard almost daily was, "I will never give you a divorce. If I can't have you, nobody will. I will kill you, kill me, and burn the house down." He had already put guns to my head, picked me up by my neck, slammed me against the wall, and choked me until I passed out. Telling him I would call the police or leave only made things worse. He watched me like a hawk.

One day, I finally made the decision to go to a church support group and there I found a great lady who I confided in. It wasn't easy; ever since childhood speaking out was a taboo, something that got me into more trouble—"How dare you say something"; "How could you embarrass us like that"; "How could you lie like that?" and so on. That day, however, I brought my folder with all the evidence I had been collecting and documenting, including all the ex-girlfriends and other people I had been talking to from his past. I handed it to her and said, "If I don't wake up alive, here is everything you need to know." I thought she would just nod and forget about me, and to my amazement this lady believed me, valued me, and called the DA's office, and literally within two hours I was under protection and they were arranging for his arrest. I was scared, amazed, relieved, and in tears, all at the same time.

Outcomes and Ahas from the Fourth Marriage

He got arrested, went to jail, and hung himself in jail, and because it never went to trial I was still labeled the liar. And guess what? I still stood up for myself and for others, broke a thirty-year cycle, and have helped thousands of other men and women realize that remaining silent serves nobody. I made a commitment to self-care and self-healing and the empowerment, inspiration, and education of others. A commitment to thrive, be a warrior.

Ahas from the Full Marriage Cycle

Did you see the patterns in the marriages? Since I grew up in what I perceived to be an unstable home and had parents that traveled a lot, I chose partners that had very close-knit families. I stayed because of the parents and tolerated the abuse because I was used to it and associated it with some sort of level of security. Oddly, when I look back now at these close-knit families I realize there was one parent that was very controlling, which explains why the child-partner I married turned out to have those rage-control issues. Of course back then I could not see that; all I could see was the families who sat together at meal times.

Everywhere I went I would adopt moms, dads, siblings, and so on, to build myself a family. Today, I consider the world my family!

Ahas for You to Think About

- Remember you are not alone.
- Speak your truth, there is always someone, somewhere

that has been waiting to hear exactly what you have to say.
- When you think you have it bad, realize there is always someone, somewhere that is having it way worse than you.
- Asking for help is not weak; it takes incredible strength.
- You are a victor, not a survivor. Survivors live in fear.
- You are not a victim. Victims live in pity.
- Make time for daily self-care.
- Make a commitment to motivate, inspire, educate others via example.
- Be authentic.
- Take time for play and laughter every day.
- Make sure to unplug from technology every night from the bedroom; make sure your bedroom is your sanctuary for sleep and self-care.

Life Ahas

I am now fifty-one years old, have had thirty-five surgeries—including a hysterectomy at the age of twenty-five from all the sexual abuse—and am now Bionic, with two new knees and two new shoulders. I have forgiven, still forgive, learned, still learn and love each and every day...

Life is a journey of patterns and ahas; you must only look for them and be open to seeing them. Once you discover the ahas you can choose to make different choices the next time. There is an old saying: "You are blind and unconscious the first time you fall into a hole or pattern, because you didn't know it was there. However, once you are aware of the hole or pattern and you still choose to fall into it, you are no longer blind—you are responsible." Once you are conscious and aware you can make the strong choice to get the help you need to break the cycle, until then you will repeat and attract the same vibrational patterns.

Life is a journey that is twisty, amazing, colorful, wet, steep, slippery, awesome; it is a never- ending question that astounds the mind-body-spirit-soul. Never, Ever, Give Up on Yourself and the Journey, it is so worth it and so are you...and if you are ever doubting that, just say to yourself, "I am BLAW—Beautiful, Loved Appreciated, and Worthy."

ABOUT THE AUTHOR: Carly Alyssa Thorne is a writer, activist, and transformation catalyst. A firm believer that life is all about sharing, collaboration and teamwork, she lives from a Paying it Forward—The Ripple Effect mentality each and every day. She spent more than twenty-five years sculpting, integrating, refining, and continually educating herself in the areas of the multi-sensory, psychology, theology, philosophy, business, multi-media, entertainment industry, nutrition, fitness, health, NLP-Neuro Linguistic Repatterning, hypnotherapy, energy healing, archetypes, Feng Shui, and eastern-western healing and medicine, all of which she combined with her life experience to create a blueprint for working with individual and corporate clients.

Carly Alyssa Thorne
Transformations Life Coaching
CarlyAlyssaThorne.com
carlyathorne@gmail.com
808-226-8103

Healing within the Silence

How I Transformed the Struggle in My Business to Attract My Tribe

Crystal A. Davis

"Why are you there?" my coach asked me as I complained bitterly about my government job. The question stopped me cold. I didn't have an answer. I thought, "You mean I have a choice?"

It was 2009. After fifteen years in the federal government, I was passionate in my work with the FBI—taking on assignments with gusto to make change for a better government and a better world. I was making six figures, yet something was missing. Many days I went to the bathroom and cried uncontrollably, often not even knowing why I was in so much pain.

Within a few weeks of my life coach asking me this powerful question, I was in an offsite with the executive team. I was a strategic planner helping executives make organizational changes...or so I thought.

I had just completed the first-ever Annual Report for the organization, with great success. So when questions of organizational structure came up, I felt compelled to offer this report as a resource.

The response I received from one of the top executives was like a punch in the stomach—painful and unexpected. "We won't make decisions based on the annual report," he said, "Rather, we will make decisions based on what WE decide here today."

Outwardly, I nodded—business as usual. On the inside, I felt rejected. My work didn't matter, I didn't matter and nothing would change no matter how hard I worked.

The Pain of Not Knowing How to Wake-up from the Nightmare

My coach's query shifted me from the painful question, "Why is this happening to me?" to the empowering question, "What can

I do about this?" Just six weeks after that offsite meeting, I registered my company, Crystal Clear Solutions. I began to study Law of Attraction and became a certified Life Mastery Consultant in April 2010. A year and a half later I took a leap of faith and left my job to focus upon my business full time. And that was when I learned the meaning of the words, "Wherever you go, there you are." Within a week of leaving my "day job," I was on my knees struggling and wondering if I would survive, let alone thrive.

I worked day and night on my company, attending every networking event I could and even traveling to attend events with my success coach. Yet, no matter how hard I worked, I made little headway. I was not attracting enough clients and most of those I did have had only enrolled with me for three months or less. Within a year, I experienced bankruptcy and foreclosure.

Knock-down, drag-out fights with God became a regular occurrence. I was furious that no matter what I did, nothing changed. I would leave most networking events, go to my car and bawl my eyes out—the same feelings I'd felt while working for the FBI still welling up within me. Leaving my job had changed my environment, but it did not change how I felt inside. I was desperate to figure out what was causing my struggles, but the answer eluded me. I just knew something was missing.

So there I was, endeavoring to build my business, to "just do it," like all the experts I hired suggested, and I was failing miserably. It wasn't all about the money, though that did play a significant role. By 2014—five years into my business—I was making over $50,000 a year, yet the majority of my clients were not fully committed to their BIG Vision and would not fully invest the time and money in "Awakening to the Crystal Clear You."

By this time, I knew my life's purpose was to awaken souls…full-on, no apologies, become-all-that-you-came-to-the-planet-to-be awake. To be your very best self and "reap the pearl of great price," as Jesus called it. Shoot for the moon and land among the stars stuff! BIG vision, clarity of purpose, and peace of mind through the Spiritual Laws (Law of Attraction, etc.) is my passion.

However, while I knew what I wanted and what my purpose is,

getting the results that I wanted was a whole 'nother story! "Just do it" and the Type A, overachiever approach that I had used while working for the government was no longer working for me.

At a 2012 conference with my mentor, Mary Morrissey, she said to the group, and to my heart, "You've placed your losses in the bank of the Universe and the Universe always pays you back with interest!" Despite all my struggle and pain, her message filled me with hope. I held onto the knowing that my pathway was unfolding perfectly, even when I didn't know how it would all come together. *Note: including the loss of my six-figure salary and my home, I had invested over one million dollars in my business and my new life!

Each time I got knocked down, I'd get up, dust myself off and remind myself that something was being birthed through me. As my struggles to attract my tribe and build my business worsened, feelings about my parents and one story in particular kept surfacing.

"The Hidden Mirror" within my "Hidden from Birth" Story

Just after eight p.m. on September 19, 1972, my siblings were watching TV when they heard a baby's cry from my parents' bedroom. They always laugh when they tell this story—how my brother (who was twelve years old at the time) and sisters (who were eleven and eight) looked at each other in confusion. They were watching a medical show and thought the cry must have come from the TV—where else would it have come from?

They were confused because no one knew I was coming; my parents had hid being pregnant. My father delivered me, removing the umbilical cord from around my neck and helping me to draw my first breath.

For me, the story was not funny; in fact, it was a source of great pain, buried within me. I am not worthy to be acknowledged and celebrated (because they did not tell anyone to celebrate I was coming), I am not good enough to spend money on (because they had me at home), and I am not important enough to keep safe and secure (because they didn't use a physician and only took me to the hospital for a check-up after I was born).

These hidden beliefs were driving my entire life. My father never said he loved us and didn't give hugs and kisses, at least not that I can remember. My mother struggled with schizophrenia; some days she'd take off on walks for hours, but most of the time she laid in bed day after day. As the youngest of four by eight years, I was alone much of the time and learned to go it alone and depend upon myself.

The hidden theme showed up in my job and in networking...manifesting as unseen, unheard, and misunderstood. I was teaching Law of Attraction, yet I wasn't manifesting what I wanted, which made my pain all the more unbearable!

As I continued to move forward, I would see how everything in my outer reality was a gift, pointing me to "The Hidden Mirror" within; this mirror would lead me to transform my limiting beliefs and, ultimately, help me find my way home to myself, my purpose, and my tribe.

Finding the Gift in the Storm

By 2014, it was crystal clear that if I wanted to thrive, I had to go deeper. Much like a great storm, everything I experienced was meant to slow me down so I could see how to fulfill my purpose and attract my tribe. My deepest pain became the northern star, leading me through the storm.

My path began to light up as I applied new wisdom and answered the core question, "What would I really love?" With my focus upon this question, I clarified and re-clarified my higher Vision and deepened my connection with and trust in the Divine. As I worked and refined my process, truth emerged from beneath the pain of my hidden from birth story.

What did I find beneath my hidden from birth story? A hidden mirror containing self-sacrifice and the need to prove myself to get love—triggered by silence.

In business, when I attracted those who struggled to invest time or money in my programs, I would fire hose them with too much information and lose them in the process.

The silence drew my deepest fear—the fear that I am not loved —to the surface for healing. The more I didn't receive love and recognition, the more I needed to prove myself. Every time I had to hold the Vision within the silence, my hidden from birth story surfaced to keep me stuck!

Underneath it all, "no matter what I do, nothing changes" reinforced the belief that I am fundamentally flawed...and I kept creating situations that reinforced these beliefs.

The solution? Find the Gift in the Storm.

By looking for the gift in the storm, I began to focus on the Vision and trust the process. I embraced the silence as a gift. For when I surrendered to the silence, God/Universe/Source would lead me home.

Starting with a focus upon what I really love, I allowed my true feelings to surface and transform. Learning how to heal myself resulted in compassion for all humanity as I could see the purpose in the path; the gift in the storm; the hidden mirror leading to one's freedom.

The hidden mirror was my inner child, screaming for me to love all of her. Imagine trying to force a three-year-old to eat her vegetables. The more I forced "just do it" and "just be positive," the more resistant she became! When I listened to my inner child, she brought the most incredible gift—freedom to completely love myself and love others!

YES, it had been *me* hiding me all along! My tribe could only see me when I could see me! As I honored my desires and allowed my true feelings, I re-focused my mind to see through the lens of love...especially how loving my parents were to me and everyone else. Now, I meet people everywhere that share with me how wonderful my parents were to them as small children and young adults because my heart is *full* of love for them!

As I surrendered to God/Universe/Source within me, I became the love that I had been seeking "out there". I forgave everyone and everything. I accepted all of me and recognized my unique gifts. I awoke to realize I am the love I had always been seeking. *I am* the love of my life! And, now I freely give love and no longer seek love for myself.

As the song goes, God blessed the broken road that led me straight to you. I arrived home not despite my journey but

BECAUSE of my journey! My "hidden from birth" story allowed me to see how my limiting beliefs masked my greatest gifts; without it, I wouldn't have gone deep enough to uncover the gifts within the silence and become my authentic self. Now I know my Soul chose my path to help me fulfill my purpose to awaken souls! After all, we can only attract and teach what we know…

The storm was over when I fully surrendered with childlike trust to embrace that what I think, say, and do matters…*I matter*! Then and only then could I shine my light and attract my tribe—as Business Strategist, Spiritual Teacher, Visionary, Entrepreneur and, ultimately, Master Healer Teacher. Today, I help my clients uncover and transform their feelings of unseen, unheard, and misunderstood into the "Been there, done that" magnetic marketing message their tribe yearns to hear.

ABOUT THE AUTHOR: Crystal A. Davis—Visionary Business Mentor and Coach—helps Spiritual Entrepreneurs struggling to turn their soul's calling into marketing that attracts their tribe. After years of feeling lost and unsure of her place in the world, Crystal left a six-figure strategic planning job with the FBI and embarked upon a spiritual journey where she struggled with networking, marketing, and making money in her business. Now she delivers her "Stand Out and Shine" Magnetic Marketing Success Transformation System™ to help her clients *"Be Brilliant. Your Rules. Your Way!"* Visit the gift page on my website for a complimentary Unique Brilliance Discovery Session.

Crystal A. Davis, MBA, CPA, PMP, Life Mastery Consultant
Crystal Clear Solutions LLC
Free Gifts: crystalclearyou.com/giftsfromcrystal
crystal@crystalclearyou.com
facebook.com/groups/attractyourtribe

Silent Presence
Angélica Amaral

It came on without warning. I went to sleep one night feeling perfectly fine, and the next morning I could not get out of bed. My entire body was wracked in pain and I had no idea why. Thus began my journey.

The first doctor I saw gave me painkillers. When several weeks passed with no improvement, he referred me to a chiropractor, a rheumatologist, and an orthopedist. I saw them all—I tried their therapies and medicines—but nothing worked. I could not go to work. I could not drive my car; when I went to the supermarket I bought only the sheer necessities because I could not lift much weight. A boy at the supermarket helped me carry the bags to the car, then a neighbor would carry those bags to the kitchen.

To go to family events I had to take painkillers, and even then I could only stay for a couple of hours before the pains got the better of me. I felt worse every day, and I spent more and more time in bed.

Sometimes it was so bad that my five-year-old grandson had to bring me water to drink, because I could not get up to go to the kitchen. Sometimes, the glass felt so heavy it was difficult to raise it to my lips. Before this situation I cooked every day; now I had to eat whatever was brought to me.

Bathing was difficult, because the water droplets caused pain when they touched my body. When I was in the car, I had to keep the windows up because the wind hurt my face. I could not get hugs because touching my skin was painful. Inside my body I had different types of pain—burning, to varying degrees—twenty-four hours a day, three-hundred-sixty-five days a year.

Through all of this, the doctors could not find any physical damage. They just kept telling me I would probably heal in a couple of weeks. Instead, it just kept getting worse and worse.

I lived on medicines—pills to wake up, pills to have energy during the day, pills to relax and sleep, et cetera. I also had several unsuccessful surgeries, and felt the doctors were "practicing" on me. It was not just physical pain, either; I had fallen into a deep depression.

When my grandson announced he wanted to celebrate his birthday in Disneyland, I was distraught. How was I going to walk all day? The last thing I wanted was to be a burden on my family, but I couldn't bear the thought of not being with them. Finally I decided to go, but with a wheelchair. I smiled the entire trip so everyone would think I was happy, but there was a lot of sadness inside me. How could I be in a wheelchair when I was only in my forties?

My condition continued to deteriorate. One day, when I got to the store, the first thing I did was see if they had motorized wheelchairs; it was one of those days when I could not take five steps in a row without resting a moment.

The doctors did eventually give me a diagnosis: Fibromyalgia, and RSD (Reflect Sympathetic Distrophya). I was told, "We cannot do more, go home, your life will end up in a wheelchair." After the shock wore off, I cried until there were no more tears. How could this be? I did not feel old, and at the same time I could not do anything. What would I do with my future, with my life?

Before I knew it, ten years had passed. When someone asks me what happened in those years, I can honestly say I do not know. I do not know what I lived and what I did not live; I do not remember. It was like I was in the middle of a dense fog that did not allow me to see anything.

There was one thing I recalled during those years, and that was getting closer to God. I had always been very spiritual and had always prayed, but one day I cried out from a place of utter weariness. "My Father, I am very tired, I cannot do this anymore. It cannot be that two doctors decide my life, my future. My God, I am in Your hands, if it is time for me to go to Your side, I accept, I accept Your will. Take me in Your hands. If it still is not my time, give me the wisdom to see what You want from me—what You want me to learn from this situation of my life, let me see what You want to tell me, My Father. Guide me to go on, to see what I need to do to heal. I want to live, God, I want to get out of this situation. There has to be something else that can help me. I know that I alone could not get out of this, but with You on my side, I will. Take me in Your hand, My God! Let me see!"

And with that, I placed myself in His arms.

I do not remember exactly when I had the dream, when God took me in His arms and helped me in those moments when the pain was unbearable. There were no words, only silence, just Him and me, He loved me and I let myself be loved by Him.

After that, new therapies began to present themselves to me. The first was Biomagnetism, in which magnets are strategically placed in areas of the body corresponding to the particular ailment. Biomagnetism brought me such great improvement—it was like a miracle! And this was only the beginning. Other modalities such as Jin Shin Jyustu, The Emotion Code, and The Body Code followed, and just as the Biomagnetism they came to me effortlessly, almost without my looking for them. I studied each one of them, taking the necessary time to learn and to practice, and eventually became certified in each of them, but not before I used them myself and became personally aware of the benefits and processes. All are wonderful and each one brings the benefit for the person who needs it.

After I had started feeling better, I decided to go to the beach. I wanted to take time for myself, to pray, to talk to God. When I arrived at the place where I was going to stay, I decided to take a bath so the next morning I could head to the beach early, before it got crowded. And that's when I looked in the mirror for the first time in ten years. I did not recognize myself! What happened? I have gray hairs! I gained weight! I have wrinkles… my skin is dry. How much I had changed during those years! I had changed inside too, and for the better. Those days were wonderful, surrounded in the sea of tenderness and love of the Father God, abandoning me totally is His hands. These unforgettable days would mark the course of my life.

One day, while lying on the bed, I asked myself, do I have pain in my neck? No. Do I have pain in my back? No. Do I feel bad? No. So why did I lie down? Without realizing it, my body had to started to heal. I was in less pain and feeling stronger and healthier.

Encouraged, I decided to focus on those moments when I felt better and could do more things. Even when I was in pain, when someone asked me how I felt I would reply, "I'm fine, I feel much better."

In addition to the therapies, I was eating healthy, praying, and walking fifteen minutes a day, which would have been unthinkable just a few weeks earlier. I shed some weight without even trying, which helped as well.

I started taking fewer medications; little by little, I did not need them. I could go out more, and people came to me to see what I was doing because I looked different. They could see the change in me, and I could tell that my health was improving.

As the days and weeks passed, people came to ask for the same therapies that I was using to heal myself. One person was telling another. I started thinking about returning to work, but where? It had been ten years—did I really want to return to the same place I had worked before becoming ill? I thought about the people who were coming to me for help, and I knew this was the path I needed to follow. I could not keep quiet, people needed to know there is hope for their physical, mental, and emotional pain. I understood how they felt, and now that I was able to walk, go out, and work, I wanted to show them it was possible to recover.

Now remembering those days, I see the whole process clearly; yes, my body was slowly dying. I can also see that God was with me always. His silent presence accompanied me at all times, especially on the hardest days, and it still does.

I realized that although there were people around me they did not realize the gravity of my situation. They wanted to help me, but they did not know how. I had to have my own experience and journey through the tunnel to the light on the other side.

Yes, I'm not the same as before. Those years strengthened me. The lived experience is unique and incomparable. I learned that I had to make my own decisions, that nobody could do anything for me to heal if I did not want it. I had to walk my own way.

I learned to have the humility to ask for help; I also learned that I had to be brave enough to take a step forward, even though it would cost me a lot of effort. Now I truly believe I did it because God always took me in His hand.

I cannot avoid crying a little when I remember those years. But now they are tears of gratitude, to God and to those wonderful techniques I found in my search for health and that now I practice to help others. Biomagnetism, The Emotion Code, The Body Code, Jin Shin Jyutsu, thank you!

I now understand that God answered when I finally placed myself in His arms, when I said, "Let me see. Guide me. Take me by Your hand!" To this day, I can still feel the vibration of His love in my soul; it makes me rise every morning full of health and love—full of His love!

ABOUT THE AUTHOR: Angélica Amaral is a certified practitioner of The Emotion Code, The Body Code, Biomagnetism, and Jin Shin Jyutsu. Always intrigued with natural healing, it was her own struggle with Fibromyalgia and Reflex Sympathetic Dystrophy—and her miraculous healing through the above modalities—that set her on her true path. Since opening her own healing practice in 2010, Angélica has witnessed the physical, mental, and emotional transformation of countless clients. Angélica is a Verified Health Practitioner of the Pastoral Medical Association. She is fluent in Spanish and English and volunteers at Sanoviv Medical Institutes in California and Mexico.

Angelica Amaral
Bioenergetics Balance
bioenergeticsbalance.com
bioenergeticsbalance@gmail.com
818-814-6484

Journey to the Dark Night of the Soul and Back

Only THE TRUTH Will Set You Free

Lisa Morgan

In 2004, I contributed a chapter to a book called *Sacred Healing*. It was called "How Music Soothed My Soul, Kept Me Whole, and Forever Preserved the Joy in My Heart." I had just begun Bioenergetics Therapy. For years, I'd been intrigued with bioenergetics, knowing that "some-day" I wanted to pursue this kind of work. I'd had a weird experience—of *losing my voice* in a workshop called "Finding Your Voice". The therapist had us experimenting and playing with voices when suddenly he said, "TALK IN YOUR *OWN* VOICE". When I opened my mouth, I was unable to utter a sound. I was shocked. This is my story—*a* fifteen-year journey into the unconscious, healing from Trauma, Sexual Abuse, Dissociation, and PTSD.

Bioenergetics is a body-oriented process that uses body-voice-energy exercises to induce "vibration." In my first session, I learned I had "trapped energy" in my stomach. I had no clue what this meant, but trusted I was in the right place to find out. Thanks to my work in hospitals, I also knew what treatment I did not want to pursue. For fifteen years, I'd observed psychiatrists in action, using "talk therapy." The results were dubious. I called it .the revolving door syndrome"—patients with repeat hospitalizations, multiple diagnoses, medications, and more medications—and I never wanted anyone to label me or numb me out. Besides, I already knew what I already knew; it's what I didn't know that I had to figure out. I used to say, "I'm not living in the past; the past is living in me." My body's always been my best friend, keeping me honest. When things don't resonate well, it lets me know.

During that first session, I said, "I just want my child's singing voice back." As a child, I played teacher/school with my dolls—first talking, then whispering, and finally in silence. I'd always wondered why I stopped talking in my own bedroom! As a teenager, I remember cruising with my friends. They'd be sitting in the front seat, singing at the top of their lungs, while I was in the back with my jaw clenched tight. I experienced a deep sadness. Why couldn't I open my mouth and join in their fun? Years later I'd revisit this grief. The angelic voices of my precious daughters-singing-triggered my heartache.

Finally, there was my career as a Music Therapist. Why on earth would a person who *hates* their voice and is a closet pianist choose an occupation that requires both skill sets? Does that make sense?

I was four weeks into the sessions when my mother died. After her funeral, I announced, *"This isn't about my child's singing voice.* I intuitively knew that the juxtaposition of therapy and her death was no accident. *This must have something to do with me and family. So, for whatever reason, I am* committed *to this process* and *wherever it takes me. Besides, I KNOW I don't have anything like sexual abuse in my history."* Little did I know that I was about to open—"Pandora's Box" and "The Dark Night of the Soul."

Five months into therapy, I achieved a "full body vibration." A surge of energy erupted, like a volcano, from deep within my core. My jaw dropped open wide, releasing bloodcurdling screams. These went on and on. Finally, I dropped to all fours, waiting for my body to be done. I'll never forget my therapist's face when I looked up; her eyes were as big as saucers. Years later she'd tell me she wasn't alarmed by my screaming, but by how long it lasted. And that was only the beginning.

I credit my infinitely curious mind; the whisperings of my intuition; and the promptings from my higher self with guiding me towards healing. *My unconscious was driving me forward.* Instinctively, I knew there had to be a reason for shattering. Extreme panic and anxiety do not come out of NO-WHERE! I used to say, "How does a person go from forty-seven years of extreme success, living full-out…to…becoming totally shut down and dysfunctional?" There had to be a ROOT CAUSE and I was determined to find it.

My body's vibration blasted through an internal block in my

root chakra (armoring), creating a palpable *swoosh* of energy. For the next three years, my body released sounds and voices—myself as fetus, baby, child, teenager, and adult; screaming, sobbing, ranting, RAGING, snarling, growling, mewing, sputtering, coughing- and more. It would take more than seven years—in bioenergetics and EMDR (Eye Movement Desensitization Reintegration)—to meet (most) of my parts. I had opened the door to my unconscious. Soul Retrieval allowed my splintered-off (dissociated) "soul parts" to emerge.

Psychiatry would call this phenomenon Dissociative Disorder (previously Multiple Personality Disorder); I call it a GOD-GIVEN GIFT–inherent in the DNA of every being. It's part of our built-in survival system—an extension of the stress response, *flight, fight, freeze, submit, and dissociate.* When a child is rendered totally helpless, overwhelmed with terror, the conscious mind *has to* split. Dissociation not only saved my life, it gave me back my life.

My parts had a job—to "STORE or HOLD" the mental pictures of abuse—and they did it extremely well. <u>I have no conscious memories of my past.</u> Instead, I developed AMNESIA, which allowed me to live full-out for forty-seven years. "My Life-Part 1" was all about EGO; building a foundation of success (my survival script). I <u>collected memories</u>—rooted in peak experiences—of vitality, creativity, exuberance, and passion. My resume was filled with accomplishments, achievements, and social accolades. All were *visceral* experiences; living "in my heart," from joy and love. GOD constructed an inner insurance policy—"a knowing" anchored in THE KNOWING—of the goodness of life. Building me up from the inside out created a reservoir of inner strength that would sustain me during the years of desperation.

Although dissociative amnesia shielded me from horrifying memories, it could not spare me the crippling after effects of trauma. With Pandora's Box open, I would <u>have to</u> FEEL THE FEELINGS of my E-MOTIONS (energy in motion) that got buried alive in my body. PTSD is a manifestation of the autonomic nervous system seeking the release of trapped energy. Panic, anxiety and depression (depressing the RAGE) are its symptoms. It's a living hell.

In his book, *Waking the Tiger: Healing Trauma,* psychologist Peter Levine describes how animals recover from a life-threatening attack. Through a naturally occurring process in which the animal makes spontaneous/involuntary movements—shaking, trembling and deep spontaneous breaths—the autonomic nervous system "resets and restores" its equilibrium. Levine had uncovered a BREAKTHROUGH distinction. TRAUMA is a FUNCTION of the NERVOUS SYSTEM—*not* an indication of psychological dysfunction—and panic, anxiety and depression are the symptoms of trauma! With PTSD, we're not losing our minds. Our body is trying to heal itself!

During my EMDR years, I was constantly triggered by anxiety and panic. I lived with stomach aches 24/7. This was "the presence" of that trapped energy; a "soul part" seeking release. I suffered a lot. I became intimately familiar with the emotional pain of suicidal patients. The feelings of despair, despondency, hopelessness, and depression overwhelmed me. I just wanted to die. I thought about hospitalization, but knew that traditional treatment would never comprehend my healing journey, especially my work with energy workers and psychic healers.

For years, I did my own release sessions at home. With tape recorder in hand, I'd lie on my bed and let my legs shake (violently). Eventually voices would emerge; sometimes sounding like my father. Through these re-enactments, I pieced together the puzzle pieces of my life *and* learned about the things my father did to me, and things he said. I always knew I lived with extreme self-hatred, but never suspected my father's words as the ROOT CAUSE. His beliefs were written on the "blank slate" of my inner child's unconscious mind. Unfortunately, I took them in, believing him. It's very cleansing to discover something that enables you to *let yourself off the hook.* Healing occurs when we're able to move from our heads to our heart, embracing our "self" with unconditional love and compassion.

I was never afraid of my process. All I wanted was to let whatever "it" was, out. In his book, *The Body Keeps the Score,* Dr. Bessel Van der Kolk refers to a patient who calls this shaking "his epileptic fits." I'm sure for others this would be terrifying.

Over time, it became apparent that most of my conscious

memories were fragments of an incident (the tip of the iceberg) <u>or</u> a "made-up story" of my inner child. IMAGINATION is an amazing survival gift. It protects the child from knowing the truth when it's too much to bear. I always believed I was "daddy's little girl" and my childhood bedroom was my "safe haven." Eventually I'd have to confront the truth—that neither of these things was true.

My bioenergetic years were an "incubation period," giving my conscious mind time to adjust to the truth. Too much/too soon would be re-traumatizing. Our unconscious mind is our best friend; designed to protect and keep us safe. It would never reveal something we couldn't handle. Over the years, my parts revisited certain incidents, each time revealing a deeper, darker piece of the puzzle. Now, I finally have all the puzzle pieces I need. I've been able to weave together a new tapestry for my life. It's BIG, BOLD and BRILLIANT!

I'd be remiss if I completed my chapter without returning to my dad. Ours' was a relationship based on a SOUL CONTRACT— my life mission to STOP GENERATIONAL ABUSE. My recordings from bioenergetics reveal the baby raging at God. "I'm just a baby; just a baby. <u>HOW CAN I DO THIS?</u> I'm just a baby. PLEASE TAKE ME HOME. I'm just a baby."

If you ever saw the movie Braveheart, you got a glimpse into my Scottish Heritage. Those were times of violence, debauchery, torture, and rape. Everything was out in the open…until it went underground. "Out of Sight" does not mean "Over and Done."

My father wasn't born an abuser. It happened because of some "thing" that happened to him. I know. We were both sexually abused by his mother. My five-year-old inner child revealed my truth through a scribble drawing *she made* with *my eyes closed.* Initially, the drawing looked like a chaotic mess. Then the images emerged—the profile of my grandmother's head and her distinct hairdo, neck, bosoms, and arthritic thumb and pointer finger. When I noticed the sexual images (vagina, clitoris and dildo), my hysterical five-year-old erupted, re-enacting "a scene" of unspeakable acts forced upon me by my grandmother.

My father was a rage-a-holic. His treatment of women was outrageous and despicable. I used up a lot of life energy studying him, trying to understand why he was the way he was. Now I understand—the compulsion of my inner child's psyche—trying to make sense of human cruelty. She sought the "resolution" of childhood trauma through slavery and Holocaust books and movies; a therapy career; and healing. What TOOK ROOT in my father's psyche were RAGE and an EXTREME HATRED OF WOMEN. His LIVE RE-ENACTMENTS of his mother's abuse, was his unconscious mind trying to make sense of her egregious acts that had violated the heart and soul of his inner child to the core.

My father never knew he was abused by his mother, nor that he abused me. He had dissociation and amnesia. In spite of everything, I never doubted his love. Yes, I suffered; we both did. My dad's "life mission" was to survive … his childhood traumas … sexual abuse and being a child of the Great Depression. He worked hard his entire life to provide (generously) for his three children and ten grandchildren. My father was a SCOTTISH WARRIOR with a BRAVE HEART—these were GOD-GIVEN GIFTS we shared in common.

ABOUT THE AUTHOR: Lisa Morgan is an author and speaker with thirty years combined experience as a Board Certified Music Therapist (MT-BC.) and Certified Life Coach (C.P.C.). However, it would be her own dramatic experience during a workshop that compelled her to investigate the missing pieces of her childhood. Her fifteen-year journey allowed her to "break the code" of her unconscious mind—understanding trauma, dissociation, triggers, the freeze response, re-enactments, soul retrieval, body memories/pain, and PTSD. Lisa's mission is to help heal suffering. She is available for speeches or trainings on "The Body as Our Biography"; "Understanding the Unconscious Mind and Repressed Memories"; "Healing from Trauma: Understanding the Stress Response" and "Dissociation: A God-Given Gift for Survival."

Lisa Morgan
314-265-3491
lovetransformstrauma.com
Lisa@lovetransformstrauma.com

Dust in the Mind
Rev. Karmynn Grimmer

"All human bodies are a thing lent by God. With what thought are you using them?" ~ *Ofudesaki III:41*

I am a Tenrikyo Yoboku (useful timber/yogi). I have come to know the truth of origin after a series of events, stretching over a lifetime of devotion. It started with dreams of past lives and the future to come, and from listening to that quiet, still voice inside. Some call this voice of your guardian angels, an "imaginary friend," Oyasama (God the Parent) or Jesus Christ.

When I was nine years old, my mother married a Jewish man. From then on, I, a baptized Roman Catholic was raised as a Jew. I was fine with this because Jesus was Jewish, but eventually I realized that a lot of otherwise loving Christians hated Jews, who they blamed for Jesus' death. I didn't know which world religion was telling the truth, so later that year, while sitting at the end of the dock near my home, I asked God to teach me through nature until I was able to have the truth revealed to me, for nature is free from man's corruption. That day I found a turtle shell at the water's edge and brought it home with me. I made a simple altar on my dresser, a heart leaf philodendron. As it grew, I grew, and vice versa.

Over time animals, insects, and plants began to come to me, always with a lesson for me to learn. Mourning Doves taught me to meditate and honor God at dawn and dusk, the way they did. I would breathe the way they sang, facing the sun. While meditating at a pond, I listened to croaks of frogs and I received my mantra. Sitting on moss in the woods with a splitting headache, I brought my awareness to the moss and it showed me how it took away pain by transmuting it into the earth.

I learned to go to the earth for healing. Running through the

Heal Thy Self

woods barefoot, I felt recharged and invigorated. Plus, the mud did wonders for feet. I would find a nice place to rest, pray and sing. I would connect to the earth via my tailbone, imagining it went deep into the molten center of the earth. I would pull the magma up into my body filling my core, out the top of my head, and covering my body. Anything unhealthy, impure, or not part of who I truly am was burned off by the magma. My aura was cleansed by it coming out the top of my head and down my body. Then a golden rain would come down from the heavens, washing away the last of the impurities. Filling and surrounding me with a nurturing, protective golden light for the day or night to come.

Years later, after I'd moved to Kauai, I was still doing this meditation every morning after my ocean yoga swim. At the end of every meditation a spirit guide would suggest I walk up the mountain to a home, do this man's laundry, and cook dinner for him. I thought this insane, because I barely knew the man and you just don't do that. But my guide insisted he had something to teach me and that he must return to the church he had left.

Every day the man would return home from work and find his dinner ready and me hanging up his laundry in the backyard. In time, he began to teach me the lessons of Tenrikyo, and when he returned to the Kapaa Tenrikyo Church, I went with him and began my training to be Tenrikyo Yoboku and Minister.

At the time, I had two broken ring fingers and casts up to my elbows. He said he was going to pray for my hands. The prayer was called a "Sazuka," and included singing and sweeping hand movements. In that moment the pain in my hands vanished! He then began to tell me about Miki Nakiyama "Oyasama." As he spoke, I realized I already knew who Miki was because she'd visited me in my childhood dreams. Now, listening to him, I cried tears of gratitude. I had finally found home.

The basic principles that Oyasama taught were universal and very beautiful. Human beings and the world were created by God the Parent to see us live a joyous life. We are all brothers and sisters on this planet, and by helping one another we save ourselves from "dust in the mind."

Dust in the mind refers to mental states that reflect on the body. Sometimes this "dust" is passed down through family lines and shows up as alcoholism, heart disease, cancer, back or knee problems, colds, mental illnesses, and so on. Some dust is rooted in past lives, while some is just how you choose to use your mind on a daily basis. Not all illnesses or injuries are from dust in your mind; some are blessings by God the Parent to lead you down a better path or to allow others to help you, which allows them to clean up their own dust.

There are four basic ways to rid yourself of dust in the mind. The first is helping others, preferably without recognition. This shows humility and sincerity. The second is prayer for yourself and for others, especially in gratitude. The third way is to give or receive a "Sazuka" healing hand prayer three times. This helps to remove the dust from the root, regardless of where it came from. The healing energy of the Sazuka comes from God the Parent, who matches the giver and the receiver's sincerity. For example, there were times I prayed for Mexican women who were very devoted to Jesus Christ. Whenever I gave them the Sazuka I became hot, sweaty, and lightheaded due to the amount of energy God the Parent was pushing through me. Afterward, they told me how amazing they felt, how they'd felt God come through me. Others said they could see or feel angels placing hands on them and whispering. *It is because she is so sincere.*

The fourth way is to return to the home of God in Tenri, Japan and go to the Jiba the spot where all life began. I had always known I had to get to Japan, but I had no idea of the miraculous healing I would receive there.

At thirty years old, I had serious health concerns. All those years of belly dancing, running track, taking people on hiking trips, and walking everywhere had taken its toll on my menisci, or cartilage in the knees. I already used a wheelchair, and the doctor told me I would be walking with braces the rest of my life. When I got to Tenri, Japan, I prayed very hard to God to get me out of my chair. I promised to be devoted to God for the rest of my life and to help others to become joyous.

Just after that I met a woman with the same knee injuries as me. I prayed Sazuka for her, and she for me. The next day we "accidentally" met again and prayed for each other. On the third day, she brought friends and I prayed for them too. Soon, people with all sorts of ailments began coming to me to pray for them; a few days later they would bring me a food basket and say, "I am cancer-free, thanks to your prayer" or "I can walk again" or "my baby's paralysis is gone." I knew it was not me; it was God the Parent matching our sincerity to remove the dust and bring the mind back to a state of joyousness. I also received a healing. Within a week of my initial prayer of devotion, I was walking, slowly at first while using my wheelchair as a walker. Now I am fine. According to a 2014 MRI, I have just minimal arthritis, and my menisci have healed!

While in Japan, I also learned how to play the koto for church services; how to do the prayer dances and how to prepare the service. I visited famous places and studied Tenrikyo literature. I also received my divine grant to give the Sazuka from the head of the Tenrikyo church. Three months later I returned to the States, vastly transformed.

It would be the Pleiadian Workbook, however, that saved my life. One day the deceased writer Amorah Quan Yin came to me in spirit and told me her book would be a great help. It was 2014 and I had started to remove entities and spirits from my clients at a rate that was very draining to me. It got especially intense during and after my pregnancy; the entities around me and my family were not always nice—sometimes they were even dangerous. Spirit spiders were biting me, and they left real marks! I was constantly taking Dead Sea salt baths and asking the angels for help. I already trusted Amorah; back when she was alive she had picked out an African crystal necklace for me, which I purchased from her website. After her visit in spirit I got her book off my shelf and started working with it again. It involves doing healings with Jesus, roses, cord removal, and destroying contracts, to name a few. The book taught me to discern between who is of the light and who is not. While destroying a contract, I had a flash of me at fourteen, stomping on a cross so I could become a witch to save my friend's mom from cancer. I had promised my firstborn to God's first fallen angel! I had forgotten all about it! Terrified, I quickly called up all of the contracts with him in this life, and all my past and future lives. There were too many contracts to hold, and they lay in a big pile on the floor. I tried to destroy them as I had done so many others per the book's instructions, but these could not be torn nor burned. Heartbroken, I began to cry. Jesus appeared to the right of me and asked if I would like His help.

"Please," I said, "I don't know what to do."

"Say I am your Lord and Savior," Jesus said, "and I will make these go away."

I realized then that He had always been there, helping me. Saving me. So I said it. "Jesus, you are my Lord and Savior," and at that moment the contracts burst into flames and burned to dust. Two soul contracts, one from my heart and the other on my son's heart, were also destroyed. My intuition flipped as well. What I thought was bad was good and vice versa. Jesus forgave me for what I had done, and the next morning an angel appeared to me. The angel touched me, and all the feelings of death, gray, and sickness left my body. I felt amazing. She then explained I had to baptize or have a Jewish baby naming ceremony for my son to protect him. I, being a Malchizedek priest, did it myself, in Yeshua's name in blessed bathwater of my tub. An angel appeared to my son and I and gave him the name Mikha'el. Amorah's book was indeed exactly what I needed. Since then my life has drastically improved.

As I continue learning more about our energetic world, I always am finding new ways to remove dust from the mind. Access Consciousness BARS, Attunements, and Ho'oponopono in particular are very effective. These days, I keep things simple. First I put up protection; then I check in with Jesus each morning and night and say a prayer for a true connection with God. After, I may receive guidance from ancestors or from Archangels like Raphael, with whom I talk about my health and how to fix it; sometimes, if instructed, I do a healing on myself. For others, I give guidance on how to use their bodies as the tool it is and the gifts they have received through it with their sincerity. Most importantly, I guide them on removing the dust from their minds so they may move forward in their lives, healthy and joyous.

ABOUT THE AUTHOR: Reverend Karmynn Grimmer is a Spirit Walker, Reiki Master Teacher, Tenrikyo Yoboku, Cosmetologist, Medical Massage Therapist, Access Consciousness BARS Facilitator, Wellness Coach, and public speaker. Her work is a devotion to God, to help this Planet and her inhabitants to raise their vibrations and grow in energetic awareness. Over time she has created a system to help her students to learn about and empower themselves, heal their past, and create a healing space for others under the guidance of Jesus. She lives just outside of Buffalo N.Y., where she works out of two wellness centers.

Rev. Karmynn Grimmer
Om Me On!
OmMeOn.com
rev.k.grimmer@gmail.com
716-262-7262

The Universe Heals Through the Heart
Michelle Goebel

I was my grandmother's golden child, her shining star. I was the only one at the center of her world. When I walked into a room, my grandmother's eyes lit up and she'd squeeze me so tight. We laughed, played, colored, and wrote poetry for each other. She idolized me, and I felt the same about her.

My grandmother had multiple illnesses, including leukemia, for which she had been receiving chemo for many years. Still, she rode four buses and walked a mile through the snow (literally!) to visit me. On sunny days, she'd walk an extra mile to the playground. She never complained about being tired, nor did she reveal how much she was suffering.

I was in college when I realized how sick she really was. Over the next few years, I watched, heartbroken, as her health steadily declined. After several strokes, she was placed in a convalescent home. Each time I visited her, I'd cry all the way there and all the way home, but I never let her see a single tear.

While she was there, we set up a "sign" that would allow us to communicate after she left the earth. Though I didn't believe that was possible, I entertained this "flaky" idea. I hoped that somehow, we could always be connected. Our time together was a treasure. Our bond eternal. No one had loved me that deeply and unconditionally. When she moved to hospice, I stayed by her side day and night. Then she passed and my heart was broken into pieces.

On a sunny morning a week later, I was driving on the Interstate 95 when out of nowhere, I saw a vision of movie screen appear, superimposed on top of the highway. On it was an image of a white truck. Then I saw images of broken glass and *felt* the glass all over my body. In an instant, it disappeared, leaving me a bit shaken. I drove to my mother's house to share this inexplicable and rather eerie experience. Her friend was there too, and as I spoke they just sat at kitchen table with bewildered expressions. Over the few weeks, other similar events occurred, and though I couldn't understand them, I somehow knew my grandmother was with me.

Eight weeks later, while I was driving to the university, I saw from the corner of my eye a WHITE TRUCK heading towards me. Quickly, I cut the steering wheel. In a millisecond, my entire life changed. My car was crushed, there was shards of BROKEN GLASS all over my body and blood everywhere. I had severe head trauma, whiplash, back, neck, and knee injuries. One eyebrow was literally ripped from my face.

I remember being nauseous and in extreme pain as the ambulance rushed me to the hospital. When we got there an ER nurse ran over to help. She took one look at my face, her jaw dropped and she let out an audible gasp of horror. My heart sunk into my stomach and I remember thinking, s*he sees injured people, EVERYDAY, so if she is reacting this way something very bad has happened to me!* I was petrified.

I was under the care of six medical professionals—two orthopedists, a neurologist, a cosmetic surgeon, a chiropractor, a physical therapist and, later, a massage therapist. I was also on five different medications, including pain meds, muscle relaxers, and anti-inflammatories. Through the fog, I heard the cosmetic surgeon saying he would need to tattoo me a new eyebrow, create one with artificial hair, or a combination of both. He then added that before we could realistically explore options I would have to heal for about five months. I stared at him in disbelief. *This is not really happening. I'm having a bad dream.*

Everything in my life came to a screeching halt. I had been working full time and trying to finish college; now, I had to leave my apartment, quit my job, drop out of school, and move back in with my family. I did not know if I would ever look normal, if my body would heal, if would be able to walk properly without pain, if my memory would improve. Before the accident, I'd had dreams of travelling the world and living an extraordinary life. Now, with a broken body, four hundred dollars to my name, and no medical insurance, I was wondering if I would even have any life at all.

Each day rolled into the next; all I did was eat, sleep, go to the doctor, sleep more, and take medication. The pain was awful, but I did not like how I felt on Percocet. The depression worsened and I suffered from anxiety and memory loss too. My reading comprehension was so bad that I'd read two sentences in a paragraph, only to forget them by the time I got to the third.

Frustrated and concerned, I asked one of the more caring and patient doctors to read to me from Physician's Desk Reference about the medicines I was taking. I learned that Percocet was NOT intended for patients with head injuries!! Furious, I demanded that this doctor give me a recommendation for another orthopedist—immediately.

The trauma also had an effect on my family, especially my mom. It seemed every time she looked at me she broke into tears. One day, while at a spiritual community center, she shared my situation with someone. The woman suggested I learn to meditate and even recommended a teacher. When we met, the teacher shared some research about how meditation helps to lower blood pressure, and it had even helped her with her grades in graduate school. At first I listened to her with a skeptical ear—I didn't have high blood pressure and healing was on my mind, not grad school!

Suddenly, I flashed back to a convention on HIV prevention I had attended several years earlier, when I was an HIV educator and philanthropy co-chair as the university. The most compelling speaker was an oncologist. He shared two stories of miraculous healings that he had witnessed with his own two eyes. , "As a doctor," he said, "this was one of the moments that I dreaded the most. The woman sitting in front of me had cancer that metastasized throughout her body. I told her there was nothing that could be done and that she had three months to live. 'I'm so sorry. Please go home and enjoy the time you have left with your family.'"

Five months later, the doctor entered the examination room and was shocked to see the woman sitting there. She looked great—

with rosy cheeks and at a healthy weight. He ordered lab tests and, sure enough, there were no signs of cancer in her body! How could this be? The woman told him that every day, she was positive, felt love in her heart and visualized the cancer leaving her body. Then doctor proceeded to tell us a similar story about the HIV patient! When he was finished, the entire room was cheering and clapping.

Remembering those stories was a real a-ha moment for me. Then I thought about how awful I still felt. About how much pain I was experiencing. About how depressed I was. And I knew what I had been doing wasn't working well enough. I thought if meditation, heart energy, and positive thinking helped those other people, maybe it could help me.

This was followed by another a-ha. It was a miracle that I had even survived the truck accident. It was also a miracle that I'd had visions about, before it happened! Could another miracle be possible for me as well?

So, I learned how to meditate deeply and practiced each day, along with a series of rituals that included visualizations and release exercises, conversing with my beloved grandmother, and praying. I also used all the knowledge I had been accumulating for over a decade about the healing power of Food as Medicine. I had no idea if any of it would work.

I had only been meditating for about a week when a major shift occurred. My mother was driving me to yet another doctor's appointment—ironically, on the same street where the truck accident occurred—and I was feeling sorry for myself. We stopped at a light and that's when a man in the wheelchair crossed in front of us. His leg was missing, replaced by a prosthesis looked that like a broomstick with a sneaker. No one was pushing his wheelchair. He was wheeling it by himself. But what struck me most was the ear-to-ear grin on his face. This man, with no one to help him was happy and smiling and LIVING his life. And this very moment, the switch in my heart and brain flipped. Somehow, I knew everything was going to be okay. No, it was going to be great. I had a roof over my head, someone to take me back and forth to appointments, my grandmother was watching me and guiding me as an angel, and I was gifted with tools and messages from the universe to help with my healing process. Suddenly my heart felt light. It was as if the depression had been physically removed from my body.

Deep in my heart, there was a knowingness at the soul-level that I would heal. I continued with my daily healing rituals. I connected to my heart energy. I felt my grandmother's love and had other mystical experiences that convinced me that she was still with me. I meditated and created ways to feel the energy move through my body to heal me.

Next, the anxiety disappeared. My head stopped hurting and I could think a little clearer. The physical pain continued to decrease as well. I felt gratitude in my heart. I started to laugh and joke again. I continued practicing. After the first month of deep meditation and my energy practices, I was completely medication-free! My neck, my back, my knees, and head had healed.

Five months later, the BIG day finally arrived. It was my appointment with the cosmetic surgeon. Throughout the whole ordeal, I had never once looked at my face. I knew from the reactions of those around me that the damage was severe, and I did not want to see it. When someone died in our family, it was a tradition to cover the mirrors, and after the accident I had asked my mother to cover them again, almost as if I was in mourning. Now, as I waited for the doctor to come in, my heart was pounding with nervousness.

As he entered the room and began examining me, I studied his expression. It looked…perplexed. My heart beat faster. Finally, he said, "Well, it looks like I don't need to do anything."

"Why would you say that?" I exclaimed, "Can't you help me? Can't you do something?"

"Don't you know what you look like?" he asked.

"NO," I said, then explained that all the mirrors had been covered and I hadn't seen my face since before the accident. Without another word, he handed me mirror, and I gripped it tightly. So many emotions were swirling inside me, as I slowly lifted the mirror to my face.

When I saw my reflection, tears immediately sprung to my eyes and began streaming down my face. They were tears of joy! I was healed—even my eyebrow had grown back! The only person who was not very happy was my attorney. The case was not as big as it could have been.

I went back to work, completed college with two degrees and honors and also did volunteer work. Little did I know that I would again need to leverage these and other natural healing tools to heal myself, or that I would be working with clients to assist them in their healing. Some have tried both conventional and natural methods—and spent lots of money—only to be disappointed. The joy I feel at being able to help them heal cannot be put into words.

The truth is, we all have the innate ability to heal—if we connect through the heart. It is the portal to the universe. Unconditional love is so strong that it can reach beyond time and space. The key is to keep seeking answers, trust that you will be able to heal, and never, ever give up.

ABOUT THE AUTHOR: Michelle Goebel is a writer, speaker, and founder of Inspired Intent. Her spiritual journey began twenty-five years ago, after a truck accident left her with severe injuries. Through meditation, energy work, and natural practices, she healed herself. Later, she earned eleven certifications in Energy Healing, Meditation, Wellness, Ayurveda, and Angel Healing. She has worked with thousands of private clients to release pain, digestive issues, anxiety, and depression. She teaches them to heal illness and injuries, and to thrive by activating their inner pharmacy and inner wisdom. Michelle has also delivered wellness programs for HBO, University of Miami Health, cancer support groups and organizations throughout the US.

Michelle Goebel
Meditation/Energy Healing/Ayurveda/Wellness
inspiredintent.com
healing@inspiredintent.com
561-376-9264

Choosing to Heal
Wanda Buckner

Sally was sure she couldn't be helped. She came to my Healing Energy Services office because a friend suggested it, not because she thought anything could be done. She matter-of-factly told me about her on-the-job injury and the resulting pains and limitations. She recounted the doctors she'd seen and the therapies she'd tried. She was on Workers' Compensation and planned to apply for Social Security Disability Insurance.

I asked Sally if she liked her job. No. Was it stressful? Yes. Did she want to work again? Sally paused. For a long time. If Sally did not want to return to work, she would not recover. Her body would support her desire and remain compromised.

When Sally weighed the pros and cons of recovering and returning to work against being painful and limited in her activities for the rest of her life, she chose to recover. Sally healed physically, mentally, and emotionally and returned to her job. She finished thirty years with the company and retired with a healthy body and full benefits.

At sixty-four, my mother experienced debilitating angina. The pain was excruciating. It doubled her over and took her breath away. Mom's primary physician sent her to a specialist. However, he could not find a cause for her intense, seemingly random, gut-wrenching pain. Mom would have to live with it. She gave up driving; she was afraid she would be gripped with pain, have an accident and kill herself, or worse yet, someone else. She quit going shopping, eating out, and visiting friends. She refused to leave the house for fear of suddenly convulsing in agony. I bought Mom stamps and stationery, accepting that she would be a shut-in for the remainder of her life.

Between the pain and the isolation, Mom felt life wasn't worth living. She decided she'd either find the answer or she'd die. Mom made an appointment at an out-of-state, highly respected, heart diagnostic center. A cardiac catheterization showed a small anomaly on her heart, a protrusion that sometimes occurred on the hearts of alcoholics. However, this anomaly was not enough to explain her pain and Mom had no history of drinking. Despite her effort, time, and expense, nothing was solved.

Assured by the cardiologist that the pain was not about her heart, Mom looked for other causes. The pain was slowly killing her—it robbed her of her appetite, her energy, her zest for life. Could it really be heartburn as others had suggested? Mom systematically eliminated foods from her diet. Within a month, she had her answer. The culprit was tea! The health questionnaires Mom filled out asked how many cups of coffee did she drink a day, how many cigarettes did she smoke, how many alcoholic drinks did she have? The answer to these was none. No one asked about tea.

Mom found out she was so sensitive to caffeine that even the smallest amount triggered severe angina. Her discovery also explained her sensitivity to many prescriptions and over-the-counter medications—the often unlisted ingredient, caffeine. After Mom gave up tea and everything else that might have caffeine in it, she lived angina free another thirty years.

Giving Away or Keeping our Power

Too often we give our power to a doctor, a naturopath, a shaman, a healer, a guru. The power to heal lies within ourselves. This is well illustrated in a reading I did for Leona about other lives she and her cat, Princess Daisy, shared. At the time of the reading, Leona was experiencing vague symptoms that depleted her energy and compromised her well-being to the point she could hardly work.

Princess Daisy recounted this life and its lessons to Leona.

I am a cat. An extraordinary white cat. I am unbelievably beautiful and pure. And I am an Oracle. Leona is the keeper of the Oracle. I don't mind life revolving around me at all. I rather like it. It's sort of a reversal. Wisdom flows through me. People come to me to hear the truth. Some come with very specific questions. Some come with more profound questions, but oftentimes I tell you, they have given away their power. The answers lie within themselves and they have given that power to me to give them answers for their lives. I do not ask for that power, but when they come to me, I give them what they ask.

The lesson of this life is not to give away your power. Leona already knows this. The answers do not lie outside of her; they lie within her. It is still good that she asks [doctors and other healers] about her condition, because each question gives more information. But you cannot gather leaves and make a tree. You have to plant the seed to make a tree. The seed is within her and it will grow. It is not outside of herself. The power is within.

Princess Daisy is right—no one can heal us but ourselves. We need the knowledge, expertise, and experience of medical and complementary providers to support our healing. But in the end, it is us who must decide to heal.

Sheldon told me he had tried everything for his incapacitating pain; he hoped hypnotherapy might help. It was increasingly difficult for him to meet clients at the work site; at times, he could barely walk. According to his doctor, his prognosis was grim and inevitable. Due to a progressive nerve disease he would experience a slow degradation of his ability to control his body leading to complete disability. The only question was whether the disease would progress swiftly or slowly.

I asked Sheldon if a physical test confirmed this diagnosis. He said, "No." The determination was based on a process of elimination considering his symptoms and his genetic heritage. As Sheldon described his attacks and when they occurred, I listened for patterns. I asked him to consider the possibility that there might be another, simpler, explanation for his symptoms. He often experienced attacks on Monday mornings. I noted that he dressed more formally during the week, including a belt and loafers. I asked Sheldon to stop wearing a belt and see what happened. I also suggested he call these episodes "incidents" rather than "attacks." The new language minimized the importance of his symptoms. After only three sessions of hypnosis, Sheldon gained control of the length and severity of his incidents. Using a keyword and light touch to the affected area, he could dissolve the pain. Some months after our last session, Sheldon wrote, "I just had to tell you, I haven't had any more incidents!"

Physicist and mathematician Stephen Hawking has a progressive motor neuron disease (ALS: Amyotrophic Lateral Sclerosis, or Lou Gehrig's) that has left him almost completely paralyzed. He has a tracheotomy and uses a voice synthesizer to speak. Hawking says he is wholly dependent on other people, but in his mind, he is free (*Stephen Hawking: Does God Exist?* Video. 2012.) Hawking is healed, even though he is not cured.

My friend Maria had cancer for a very long time. She went through agonizing treatments that left her exhausted. Sometimes the cancer was in remission, sometimes it wasn't. Many times, she thought she would die. Many times, she wished she would die. But she didn't. Instead, Maria fell in love. When she fell in love and enjoyed living, despite her recurring bouts of illness, she healed. For the remaining months of Maria's life, she lived fully and loved fully. In the peace and joy of love, she died—healed, but not cured.

Cured or Healed or Both?

Healing is influenced by the demands of our lives; the support of those we love; our attitude about our situation; and our view of life, death, and life after death. If we believe our lives extend beyond this realm, death may feel less final and may even be welcome. If we believe we will be punished throughout eternity unless we conform to the requirements of our religion, then our time living will be consumed by fulfilling those demands. If we believe our lives end with our physical bodies, we are pressured by having only one opportunity to get it right. If we believe our illness is a punishment for a deed done in this life or a past life, that is the framework from which we will experience our illness and the framework from which we must be healed.

Elizabeth is waiting to die and has been for some years now. She has outlived her husband, her siblings, and her peers. Her home is comfortable, her family loving, and her care excellent. She has no life-threatening disease. She lives in an adult retirement community with a full program of activities. Her lunch and dinner are provided. Light housekeeping keeps her apartment tidy. When asked if she is happy, she says, "No." If asked if she'd rather be dead, she says, "Yes."

Jacqueline, Elizabeth's sister, wrote to tell her how happy she was in her new apartment—there were lots of activities, she didn't have to cook or even make the bed. Jacqueline couldn't believe her good fortune. "How did I get so lucky?" The two sisters are in the same situation, but their outlooks are different. If Elizabeth saw the blessings in her surroundings and the beauty in the details of her day, perhaps she would heal.

The placebo effect is a prime example of self-healing. We swallow a sugar pill and believe we will be healed and we are. The mechanism through which this happens is of great interest to scientists and doctors. A 2008 Harvard placebo study treated volunteers with IBS (irritable bowel syndrome) with sham acupuncture using needles that did not penetrate the skin. Even so, forty-four percent of participants reported relief of their symptoms. When combined with "attentive, empathetic interaction with the acupuncturist," 62% reported relief. (*Harvard Health Letter*. Harvard Health Publications: Harvard Medical School. April 2012.) Deepak Chopra in *Quantum Healing: Exploring the Frontiers of Mind/Body Medicine*, 1989, reports multiple stories of miraculous healings and the ability of people to self-heal. Dr. Joe Dispenza, in *You are the Placebo*, 2014, discusses and advocates using mind over body to heal. He gives many examples of people who successfully healed using his mind/body techniques.

"The body heals itself. This might seem to be an obvious statement, because we are well aware that wounds heal and cells routinely replace themselves. Nonetheless, this is a profound concept among CAM systems because self-healing is the basis of all healing." (Marc S. Micozzi, *Fundamentals of Complementary and Alternative Medicine [CAM]*. 2011.)

Choosing Healing

To be cured is to be rid of a specific disease or condition. To be healed is to be at peace with ourselves and the universe. We cannot always be cured, but we can always be healed. A young woman confided to me that her male friend had Stage 4 metastasized cancer. He was doing all the possible medical treatments as well as positive affirmations, meditation, and mental imagery. But the cancer marched on. She asked, "Why isn't it working?"

If our obsession with being cured blots out everything else, we lose opportunities to live fully in the days we have. Death is inevitable. However, even faced with a life-ending disease, we can heal. We can use the days to review our life, to express gratitude, to mend relationships, to see friends and family, and to complete whatever seems unfinished. In the time we have, whether moments or years, we can use our breath to love and appreciate this world and those around us.

When we are ill, we can choose to treat or not to treat our condition. We can choose western, eastern, alternative, or complementary interventions or use any of these methods in various combinations. To choose one type of intervention does not eliminate all others. We can choose and choose again. Sally chose to return to work. Mom refused to accept that nothing could be done about her pain. Sheldon let go of the doctor's diagnosis and allowed another possibility. Hawking accepted the restrictions of ALS. Maria chose to heal, though she could not be cured. The most important choice we make is the decision to heal. All else follows.

ABOUT THE AUTHOR: Wanda is a gifted healer, clairvoyant, medium, and interspecies communicator/instructor. Whether your needs are physical, emotional, mental, or spiritual, Wanda's work allows you to clear what doesn't support you, find your own knowing, and discover new possibilities. You truly can repair your past, heal your present, and embrace your future. More information is in her book, *Choosing Energy Therapy: A Practical Guide to Options for People and Animals.* Wanda's latest publication in *The Gifts of Grace & Gratitude* chronicles her experiences healing into life after the death of her partner due to a medical error. Wanda practices in Olympia WA and at a distance anywhere.

Wanda Buckner, EdD, Reiki Master/Instructor
Healing Energy Services
HealingEnergyServices.com
wanda@HealingEnergyServices.com
360-491-3187

About the Authors

**Are you inspired by the stories in this book?
Let the authors know.**

**See the contact information at the end of each chapter
and reach out to them.**

They'd love to hear from you!

Author Rights & Disclaimer

Each author in this book retains the copyright and all inherent
rights to their individual chapter. Their stories are printed herein
with each author's permission.

Each author is responsible for the individual opinions expressed
through their words. Powerful You! Publishing bears no
responsibility for the content of the stories by these authors.

Acknowledgements & Gratitude

THANKS. It seems such a small word to express our gratitude and appreciation for the many incredible individuals who have graced our lives and shown up divinely and purposefully to bring forth this book. A small word, indeed, and yet we deliver it with love, joy, and affection.

To our authors, your willingness to share some of the deepest parts of yourself to assist others is a selfless and amazing gift. Each of you is a remarkable example of courage and compassion in action, and we are happy to support your purpose and your work. You are a blessing.

To our team—you know who you are—we thank you for your constant support, expertise, guidance, and love. They say it takes a village, and we are truly grateful that you're part of ours. We love you.

To our editor, Dana Micheli, we thank you for your professional and compassionate insights, your time and commitment, and the beautiful energy you share with our authors.

To our trainers, Linda Albright, Kathy Sipple, and AmondaRose Igoe: We thank you for sharing your expertise, experience, and enthusiasm with our authors. By assisting them to get their message out into the world, you are helping more people than you can imagine. You're all rock stars!

To Dr. Ina Nozek who wrote the foreword for this book, we thank you for your devotion to assisting others to be their best selves, and live happy, healthy lives. We are grateful for your friendship and loving presence.

To our friends and families, we are grateful for your support, guidance, and love. Our connection makes life more beautiful. We love you.

And lastly, we are grateful for the many freedoms we enjoy, our Divine connection, and the inspiration we find all around us. We are forever grateful for this life.

Namaste` and Blessings,
with much love and deep gratitude,
Sue Urda and Kathy Fyler

About Sue Urda and Kathy Fyler

Sue and Kathy have been friends for 28 years and business partners since 1994. They have received many awards and accolades for their businesses over the years and continue to love the work they do and the people they do it with. As publishers, they are honored to help people share their stories, passions, and lessons.

Their pride and joy is Powerful You!, which they know is a gift from Spirit. They love traveling the country producing meetings and tour events to gather women for business, personal, and spiritual growth. Their greatest pleasure comes through connecting with the many inspiring and extraordinary women who are a part of their network.

The strength of their partnership lies in their deep respect, love, and understanding of one another as well as their complementary skills and knowledge. Kathy is a technology enthusiast and free-thinker. Sue is an author and speaker with a love of creative undertakings. Their honor for and admiration of each other are boundless.

Together their energies combine to feed the flames of countless women who are seeking truth, empowerment, joy, peace, and connection with themselves, their own spirits, and other women.

Connect with Sue and Kathy:
Powerful You! Inc.
239-280-0111
info@powerfulyou.com
PowerfulYou.com
PowerfulYouPublishing.com
SueUrda.com

Powerful You! Women's Network
Networking with a Heart

OUR MISSION is to empower women to find their inner wisdom, follow their passion, and live rich, authentic lives.

Powerful You! Women's Network is founded upon the belief that women are powerful creators, passionate and compassionate leaders, and the heart and backbone of our world's businesses, homes, and communities.

Our Network welcomes all women from all walks of life. We recognize that diversity in our relationships creates opportunities.

Powerful You! creates and facilitates venues for women who desire to develop connections that will assist in growing their businesses. We aid in the creation of lasting personal relationships and provide insights and tools for women who seek balance, grace, and ease in all facets of life.

Powerful You! was founded in January 2005 to gather women for business, personal, and spiritual growth. Our monthly chapter meetings provide a space for collaborative and inspired networking and 'real' connections. We know that lasting relationships are built through open and meaningful conversation, so we've designed our meetings to include opportunities for discussions, masterminds, speakers, growth, and gratitude shares.

Follow us online:
Twitter: @powerfulyou
facebook.com/powerfulyou

Join or Start a Chapter for
Business, Personal & Spiritual Growth

powerfulyou.com

Powerful You! Publishing
Sharing Wisdom ~ Shining Light

Are You Called to be an Author?

If you're like most people, you may find the prospect of writing a book daunting. Where to begin? How to proceed? No worries! We're here to help.

Whether you choose to write your own book, contribute to an anthology, or be part of our how-to book series, we'll be your guiding light and biggest supporter. If you've always wanted to be an author, and you can see yourself partnering with a publishing company that has your best interest at heart and with expertise to back it up, we're the publisher for you.

We provide personalized guidance through the writing and editing process. We offer complete publishing packages and our service is designed for a personal and optimal authoring experience.

We are committed to helping individuals express their voices and shine their lights into the world. Are you ready to start your journey as an author? Do it with Powerful You! Publishing.

Powerful You! Publishing
239-280-0111
powerfulyoupublishing.com

About Dr. Ina Nozek

Dr. Ina S. Nozek, D.C., (Ret.), M.S., CN is a retired Doctor of Chiropractic and a Clinical Nutritionist and holds a Masters degree in Human Nutrition. While in active practice, Dr. Ina had an expertise in stubborn weight loss, nutritional detoxification and women's health issues. Dr. Ina currently serves as Product Expert and Field Trainer for Isagenix International. She has also been the nutritional consultant and columnist for several holistic health publications. Her personal story is featured in the Amazon #1 bestselling book, *Women Living Consciously*. She and her husband also have recently co-authored their book, Trusting Your Inner Physician: Practical Prescriptions to Live a Life of Optimal Health, Abundant Wealth and Total Freedom.

Dr Ina has been involved in nutrition & holistic health since the mid-eighties. In addition to lecturing nationwide on a variety of health topics, she has also made numerous radio and television appearances including being the co-host (with her husband) of a 12-part cable TV series on alternative medicine and holistic health entitled "Lifeline" and together co-hosting a weekly radio health talk show entitled "Listen for Your Health." She and her husband owned & directed the Lifeline Center for Holistic Health in Toms River, NJ from 1988-2004.

She lives on the Jersey Shore in Toms River, NJ and is a very proud Mom of 3 children; Max, Arielle, & Jacob.

Dr. Ina Nozek, DC, MS
Clinical Nutritionist/Weight loss expert
Author, Speaker, Success Coach
Drinanozek.com
Physiciansonamission.com
732-300-1925

May You Live Each Day
Open to Possibility...

And May You
Heal Thy Self!